THE (EXPANDED)
FREELANCER'S RULEBOOK

Bonnie Hearn Hill

The (Expanded) Freelancer's Rulebook

STORY LINE PRESS
ASHLAND, OREGON

Published by Story Line Press, Three Oaks Farm, P.O. Box 1240, Ashland, OR 97520-0055, www.storylinepress.com.

This publication was made possible thanks in part to the generous support of the Nicholas Roerich Museum, the Andrew W. Mellon Foundation, and our individual contributors.

Author photo by DiMarco
Cover design by Lysa McDowell
Interior design and composition by
Valerie Brewster, Scribe Typography

LIBRARY OF CONGRESS
CATALOGING-IN-PUBLICATION DATA

Pending

Hearn Hill, Bonnie
p.   cm.
ISBN 1-58654-012-2

To Larry Hill,
who took the class,
married the teacher,
and never lost faith in this book.

ACKNOWLEDGMENTS

I'm grateful to my editors, especially Fran Hodgkins, who made me sound good when I wasn't, and who never left fingerprints. My gratitude to Blue Dolphin Press for hiring me as a columnist and publishing the first Rulebook under the guidance of Leann Zotta; to Paddy Calistro and John Lewis, who are living proof that the term, "kind editor" is not an oxymoron; and to the SouthWest Writers and Mendocino Coast writers' conferences, for helping me launch my speaking career. Most of all, my love and appreciation to my students, who have taught me as much as I have taught them, and who have enriched my life beyond belief.

Contents

THE (EXPANDED)
FREELANCER'S RULEBOOK

What This Book Can Do for You, & What It Can't

Never make excuses, never let them see
you bleed, and never get separated from your baggage.
WESLEY PRICE, *Three Rules of Professional
Comportment for Writers*

Every day of every year, countless freelance writers spend their time and money at bookstores, conferences, seminars and Web sites trying to answer one recurring question. What do publishers want? What they find is conflicting, self-serving, and sometimes just incorrect information.

You're told you can make $80,000 a year as a freelancer. You're encouraged to forget about money and cherish the process. Often you're served up rehashed information that might have once been accurate. What you're reading is philosophy. What you need are rules.

When searching for a text for my beginning writing class, I came upon a new book by a published writer purporting to share the secrets of freelancing. I glanced at the introduction, then decided to check the author's knowledge in two telling areas: multiple submission and query letters. In these and several other critical areas, he reiterated generally accepted but incorrect information that is passed along only to keep beginning writers out, not let them in. It's no wonder that most writers learn the way I did, by trial and error, primarily error.

Do you have any idea how many freelance submissions are rejected? Based on what editors and agents have shared with me, approximately ninety-eight percent. Do you have any idea why? Because most of them are not that well written and not suited for the publication to which they are submitted. Your fresh idea, your targeted query are treading water in the slush pile, waiting to be noticed.

Of the approximately thirty people in my advanced writing class, more than ninety-five percent have gone on to sell their writing. (That's about twenty-eight and a half people, so I've obviously based it on an average.) At this writing, all of my advanced students are published writers. Some may have published essays in the local newspaper or articles in trade publications. Others have published with top magazine market. A few have sold books—one for a six-figure advance. The point is that these people, from very different backgrounds, reached their writing goals, and they beat the numbers game. They might not write any better than you do, but they know the rules.

Throughout my early freelancing days, I fantasized about working as an editor, just until I figured out how their minds worked, I thought, not long enough to do any serious damage to my creativity. I began my current editing position in 1982, and in the first six months, I learned more about the editorial perspective than I had in the first ten years I struggled as a writer.

This book is the result of more than twenty years of working with freelancers. Its purpose is to save other writers the years

I wasted trying to learn the rules. If you need a book that will teach you the craft of writing, you'll discover many fine ones elsewhere. This is not a book about how to write. It's a book about how to sell.

When I became serious about writing for publication, I found conflicting information, self-serving or uninformed teachers, and overpriced promises guaranteed to teach me how to write my way to a six-figure income. The first books I read were the ones that promised to make me rich. I figured that if I could earn just a fraction of the promised income, I would be able to spend my time writing about subjects that interested me, without having to worry about the mundane realities of food and shelter.

Payment for my first article back in the early 1970s was approximately seventy-five dollars. So much for getting rich. It was only after I became an editor and began working with freelancers that I understood why so many fail. By observing the process from the editor's side of the desk—with the head of an editor and the heart of a writer—I learned the rules. And I followed them as I built a successful freelancing career.

Can I, like those carnival-barker writing coaches, claim to teach you how to make a six-figure income by writing just two hours a day? Not even. You may not want to crank out copy for 900 numbers and mail-order companies, and even if you do, you're still going to have to learn the rules to establish and build upon a relationship with your prospective editors.

Can I, then, teach you how to forget the commercial aspects of publishing and focus on the Process, capital P, maybe even convince yourself that's all you want (or should want) from writing and from life? Absolutely not.

Publication will validate you faster than anything. Selling your work, for even the smallest of sums, is essential to your self-esteem, and it's your first step toward a career as a writer. Until that happens, you'll find yourself paying too much attention to the doubtful voices of friends and family, as well as and perhaps especially, those in your own head.

The process of creation, exhilarating as it can be, is distinctly separate from the process of publication. The first is a gift with no strings and no rules. The second is hard work, with many rules, most of which have not been written down. Creativity is like money. We're rich with it; we spend it in ways that give us pleasure, but ultimately we need to know, at the very least, how to keep track of it. If we are to be published, we must deal with someone's rules, and that someone has a major say in our success.

So, I can't guarantee to make you a millionaire, or even a six-figure-naire. I can't show you how to feel superior and cerebral about being unpublished. What I can teach you is how to approach and establish relationships with editors, thus saving yourself considerable time. I can show you how to think like an editor, how to approach an editor, how to earn that editor's respect, again and again, regardless of what you write or where you want to publish. And, unlike most of the information I see on the market, I can and will tell you the truth as I know it, even on controversial subjects.

Who Needs Rules?

When I asked one of my editors if she had any advice for the readers of this expanded rulebook for freelancers, she said, in the frosty New England accent she usually reserves for strangers, "That's easy. Just don't write your query in crayon, and you'll be ahead of most of them."

Okay, maybe my friend was having a bad day. Then again,

maybe the past-deadline cover story that hadn't arrived and the complaints about inaccurate facts in an article she had published last month were contributing to that bad day. Both of these problems, and others I will mention later, were created by free-lance writers she had trusted with assignments.

These professional freelancers know the rules, don't they? The caller who left the long-winded query on the editor's answering machine knows the rules, doesn't he? The e-mail writer whose many attachments took twenty minutes to download knows the rules, doesn't she? You, I—we all know the rules. Don't we?

We read the trade magazines. We study the market listings. And maybe that's part of the problem. The trial-and-error approach incurs enough frustration to drive a sane person into something dependable, like insurance sales.

Another part of the problem is the writer. Many don't realize that they need to know the rules until it's too late. She lands an assignment then can't locate her sources in time to make deadline. He sells an article but fails to negotiate payment. You receive close-but-no-cigar rejection letters. Something is wrong with either your query or your ideas, you know. But how do you find out what? If you have similar concerns, this book may be for you.

Another Rulebook?

In 1997, at the request of a magazine editor for whom I frequently worked, I wrote *The Freelancer's Rulebook*, a twenty-eight-page guide for freelance writers. Because of the space limitation, I was able to include only the most basic rules, the ones I thought would be most difficult for a writer to learn on his/her own.

The booklet is still selling. I continue to receive e-mail questions from editors and writers all over the country, and a few from other countries. These questions further point out to me how difficult it is for writers, whatever our level of expertise, to learn the unwritten rules of freelance writing. They also point out to me the areas of greatest concerns to freelancers. Those are the areas I will cover in this expanded version.

When she first described the concept of this book to me, my editor wrote, "This should end up being a booklet that you would give to any writer who wants to work for you. The book should be *your* rules, written from *your* experience — things that work, things that don't."

I've done my best to make it that. On some issues (business cards, ellipses, SASEs, the dreaded squirrel stickers), I probably sound like a stuffy editor. On other issues, multiple submission, for instance, I side with the writer and tell the truth most writers suspect and most editors don't want to hear.

At all times, I have tried to approach these rules from both sides of the desk, as a fellow freelance writer who happens to work as an editor. My day job has provided me with the information I needed when I started freelancing. I know why approximately ninety-eight percent of freelance submissions fail because I've been forced to deal with those failures almost every day since 1982. I know what an editor needs, wants and ignores, because it's what I need, want and ignore when I'm at my day job.

At the end of each chapter, you'll find a listing of the rules covered therein, sort of a mini index, in case you're seeking advice on a specific area of freelancing.

Along the way, I'll also toss in exceptions to the rules, because, as you probably already know, freelancing is not a paint-by-number business, and if an experienced writer feels like breaking a rule, he or she may well have a reason for doing just that.

Assumptions about You

I'm assuming here that you're a freelance writer, published or otherwise, who'd like to sell more consistently and to better markets. I'm also assuming that you already know how to write, that you own and know how to use a dictionary and style book and that you care enough about your career to read and study trade publications for writers.

These rules are intended to help you establish and maintain professional relationships with those editors for whom you want to work. Break one or two, and it probably won't affect your career one way or the other. Break all or most of them, and you'd better be considerably more talented than any other freelancer submitting on any given day.

In Search of the Secret

When I first began teaching and speaking at conferences, I learned immediately that writers are seeking The Secret, that one something that will change their lives and make them *real* writers. I see it in their eyes and feel it in the expectant silence of the room. When contracting for a speaking engagement at a major writers' conference, I told the director that I wanted to talk about the realities of the writing business.

"We already tried that," he said, "and that isn't what the people who attend these things want to hear. Go glitzy with it. Tell them how to sell to Hollywood and make a million."

Although I couldn't provide what he requested, I understood that the director thought he was satisfying the attendees' needs by giving them The Secret. What his version of The Secret lacked in veracity, it would make up for in hope, the one drug every writer needs like air. I thought about my version of The

Secret. What had I conveyed to the students in my workshops and seminars that helped them find success or at least manage to go on to the next article or story, the next paragraph?

This is probably the most important thing I tell them, The Secret, according to me.

It's doable.

I don't like that word, but it's as close to The Secret as I can come. It's not a cheer-leading, "You can do it," because I don't know you. But I do know this business, and I am comfortable telling you that writing for publication is doable. And since there's almost always a qualifying *if* attached to such positive statements, here's mine. It's doable, *if* you know and choose to follow the rules.

The First Five Rules

1. Don't expect any book, mentor or guardian angel — regardless of what they promise or how much you pay them — to teach you how to make millions as a writer.

2. Know that most writers who sell on a regular basis do so because they have learned the rules of connecting with and working with editors.

3. Learn how to write. Invest in and practice using a dictionary and style book.

4. Try to aim for paying markets. Writing is a business. You're providing a product, and you need to be paid for it.

5. Expect hard work as the price you pay for being a writer, and don't give up. Selling your freelance writing is (there's that word again) doable.

_____

What's Next?

You don't really have be an editor to know what's expected. You need only *think* like one. Here's how.

CHAPTER I

The Editorial Mindset

What is true of friendship
is true of editing; the understanding
must be continually refreshed.

EDWARD WEEKS

B efore she left her position as editor of *Cosmopolitan,* the magazine she had virtually created thirty-three years before, Helen Gurley Brown agreed to an interview with me for an editorial trade magazine. Her style and her proactive approach to publishing had once help me shape my own career choice. I asked how she had managed, after all those years, to stay tuned to the needs of her much younger readers. "Emotions don't change," Brown said. "I didn't have to go through her mind, her body and her soul with a can opener to know what she was going through."

Of course not, I thought. If you understand your reader's emotions, you know her needs.

Your first reader—the one you must convince that you are worthy of a larger audience—is the editor to whom you hope to sell. You don't need Brown's proverbial can opener to know this person's needs. Just mentally put yourself in her job; understand her emotions, which are probably very different from yours.

At one of my freelancing jobs, I outlasted four editors in less than two years. "You're lucky," the fourth one told me. "The politics never make it to the freelancer. We're the buffer."

He was right. The editor had to worry about budget, but I got paid whether he was over or under. He did indeed have to concern himself with office politics. I had only to get him what he needed, when he needed it, and with the agreed-upon number of words.

I did just that, and because I understood his needs, I told him that if he ever got stuck at the last minute, I would do what I could to help him. He thanked me, and he did take me up on that offer. Boy, did he take me up on it. My eyes still burn recalling all those nights peering at a computer screen while the rest of my household sanely slept. At one point, with a two-day turnaround (which by then I had begun calling a "seven-eleven"), I pondered the wisdom of my original promise.

Later, after some sleep of my own and another grateful e-mail from my editor, it occurred to me that this magazine was listed in every major marketing source book. It paid well and, just as important, on time. The editor probably had a mountain of manuscripts on his desk full of publishable ideas from freelancers as or more qualified than I. Why did I get the assignments time and again? Because I knew how he thought. I'd proven that I understood his needs, and he felt comfortable trusting me to come through with difficult assignments, even at the last minute when an assigned author backed out.

Publications purchase freelance submissions for numerous reasons, ranging from a small staff to a need for fresh voices.

Whatever the reason, we editors and writers need each other. You'd never know that to hear what we say about each other though. When I'm with my freelancer friends, they complain about how long editors take to respond to their queries. They grouse about slow pay and impersonal communication.

When I'm with my editor friends, they complain about how long writers take to complete their assignments. They grouse about low salaries and budgets and how their workloads cheat them of the time they'd like to spend developing relationships with promising freelancers. It all depends on which side of the desk you're sitting. You're on the writer's side right now, but perhaps it's time to change perspective.

If you're a dependable writer who can deliver what you promise, you will find an editor, probably more than one, who will feel lucky to work with you. This book will cover how to make that contact and nurture that connection. First, though, try putting yourself on the other side of the desk.

An Editor Thinks *Time*.

We editors measure out our lives in deadlines. While my friends are enjoying football games and autumn leaves, I'm wondering how to make one more holiday décor story appear fresh.

When you're assigned a deadline, don't say, "That's my Uncle Howard's birthday. We're planning a big party in Dubuque." (I swear to you, people really do make equally unwise remarks.) Say, "I can handle that," and be sure you mean it. Uncle Howard will love you just as much when you visit the following weekend, and you'll love yourself even more for being a finisher.

Most freelancers, this one included, would lead less-complicated lives if they remembered that the deadline is the last possible moment to submit the article. Your editor will not be unhappy if you submit it sooner.

Unfortunately, as you may already have experienced, there's this nasty little adrenaline rush that kicks in the closer you get to deadline. A writer friend of mine calls it "deadline addiction." Suddenly, the piece comes into focus. You're energized and excited, unable to leave the computer for a moment. And with good reason, since the deadline is probably looming.

I'm the last person to hypocritically lecture you about avoiding a relatively harmless high, and deadline addiction can be just that. However, if you put off the piece too long, you run the risk of losing your notes, or worse, your enthusiasm. The adrenaline departs, leaving you with a dull, aching head and the blank pages of procrastination.

My rule is to start writing while the notes from the first interview are still warm. That provides the loose structure to which you will add as you complete other interviews. Even if you finish the piece at the last minute, you're really focusing and polishing, not trying to create something out of thin air.

An Editor Thinks *Space*.

When you say the article will run fifteen hundred words, that's what the editor will expect—and plan for. Don't submit two thousand words with a breezy note to "take out what you don't like."

I've written one book and dozens of articles on the importance of focus, and I won't dwell on it here. Suffice it to say that just because it's a brilliant sentence doesn't necessarily mean it belongs in your article. Just because the source you interviewed said it, and you wrote it down, doesn't qualify it for membership in your published article. I've had to kill wonderful anecdotes and quotes, telling myself they'll work in some future, as-yet unassigned article, just so that I could get them out of the current one.

Force yourself to cut everything that doesn't contribute to the overall focus of the piece. It's a nasty little task, isn't it? That's why you don't dump it on your editor, who is expecting, at the very least, clean copy.

Perhaps your problem isn't too many words but too few. Maybe you overestimated how many pages your notes would cover. Now that's scary. Cutting, difficult as it can be, ranks far above trying to create copy from thin air.

I still cringe when I remember one of my early interviews with a Big Celebrity. BC didn't get back to me when he'd promised, and I didn't have the nerve to call back and pin him down to a time.

Interviewing BC was as difficult as scheduling myself into his life. I'd ask a question and get a polite, British, "yes," "no," and occasionally an "indeed." I knew I was in trouble when halfway through my list of questions, I'd taken fewer than two pages of notes.

Recalling that interview is still painful. I've read the resulting article, only once, just to see if it is really as unfocused as I thought. It is, of course. I was forced, in my desperation, to include every phrase and sentence that poor BC uttered. I quoted from his books and books written about him. I stretched and struggled, and if I learned anything from the experience, it's plan for the worst-case scenario.

You can't predict if someone is going to be a nice person but a lousy interview. You can, however, do some research in advance to cover your proverbial in case the interview gets scary or your

BC drops out entirely, leaving you to interview secondary sources. What has your source written? Where quoted? Where written about? Can he or his publicist send you a press kit? Photos? I'm always amazed at the way fluffy press-kit verbiage can look like Shakespeare reincarnated when I'm on deadline and my major source fizzles.

This information can also help you send along to your editor suggested sidebars and boxes as convenient and helpful ways to fill some of the space you failed to. Since they actually have a function, you are not cheating either the reader who bought the magazine or the editor who bought your article.

An Editor Thinks *Completion*.

Most editors are hard-working professionals, who in spite of their jobs, still possess great love and respect for the written word. As much as we dislike having to reject promising manuscripts, we lack the time to teach everyone with potential what it takes to edit that raw material into published words.

You may have looked at published articles and said to a friend or yourself that famous phrase, "I can do better than that." I know people who used those very words as the motivation to write and sell their own articles and books. I know many others who miss the point. These people criticize, and often quite colorfully, what they hate about the travel article in the local newspaper or the essay in the back of their favorite magazine. They see what doesn't work, but they seldom see what does.

These are often the same people who criticize popular novels as being stupid and predictable, without seeing the craft that make such books achieve the goals the author set out for them. You can learn from even a bad book, a poorly written article.

Remember, it's in print for a reason. Don't dwell on what's wrong with it; try to find out what's right. That quality may be what got it published, and it may even be the quality your writing lacks.

When I was writing a wine article, I enlisted the help of a friend who is an expert on the subject. My friend explained that the wine we were discussing was "complete." It wasn't brilliant; it didn't have the nuances of a more expensive vintage, but it delivered everything a wine should deliver, at a reasonable price. It was complete, in the best sense of that word.

The *complete* story you may disparage in print has a far better chance of making it to print than the stream-of-conscious masterpiece, bathed in your very best prose and going nowhere. In order to sell, you must provide a complete, well-focused product. Even though editors may admire the potential of various writers, the demands of our jobs force us to work with freelancers who can give us what we need with minimal reshaping. That means complete stories, not promising ones.

An Editor Thinks *Dependability.*

Every editor I know has a freelancer he or she can call in a pinch when a writer fails to come through with an assignment or when we need someone who can handle a difficult subject or interview. Through experience, we learn who can meet deadlines, who has the most original ideas, and who would crawl through a snowstorm to provide the job that was promised. You can demonstrate, from your first encounter, that you're such a person.

As you build your relationship with the editor, you will become the one who can be trusted with the difficult assignments and rewarded with the good ones. That editorial need for dependability is one reason you see the same writers in print over and over in the same publications. Your ideas might be as good or better, but you can bet that these people have earned their way into the editor's mental Rolodex.

You'd probably have to work as an editor to believe this, but many writers freeze once they get the assignment. They can handle rejection, but acceptance, well, how could they possibly incorporate all that success into their lives? It really is something like that, I think. The would-be writer hears success knocking at the front door and runs out the back. Or he draws a big bulls eye on his foot, points the gun and fires.

A friend of mine who recently began working for a book publisher said she is amazed at the number of writers who never deliver once they've contracted for a book. One writer, with not a single previous publication credit, sent the publisher eight single-spaced pages of revisions for a contract. The publisher, who is a fair and writer-friendly type, said he would agree to some of the requests, but most were outrageous. Couldn't they reach a compromise?

The writer responded, "It's my way or the highway." The last anyone heard, it was still the highway, and he was still unpublished, which is probably the way he really wants it.

Was it Woody Allen who said ninety-eight percent of success is showing up? Too many writers haven't figured that out, or even if they have, they are unable to follow through. You can imagine how this delights the editor who trusted that writer with an assignment. Deadline nears and passes, the excuses start flying, and the writer's answering machine goes on.

Once you're on pretty firm ground with an editor (you've completed several assignments and gotten a go-ahead on phone interviews), you might try calling just past your deadline date.

Ask the editor if she liked your piece and if there's anything else she needs you to do. If you've already built trust with the editor, you could be rewarded with a last-minute assignment.

Now that you better understand the editorial mindset, you can begin to develop your own freelancer's mindset, which is simply a response to your editors' biggest concerns. They need the material on time? Get it in early. They need it complete? Edit yourself (with a little help from Chapter 4). Provide the best job you can, as quickly and as professionally as possible, and just as important, try to second guess your competition, that silver-tongued devil who possibly didn't come through in time or at all.

Is it always this easy? On a good day, yes. Working smart during the good days will help you work smart during the less-than-good ones. And it will help you store up credits for that long, cold winter ahead.

The Next Six Rules

6. Put yourself on the editor's side of the desk. What are your needs now?

7. Go for the deadline, even if it's ridiculous and conflicts with earlier plans. Remember that most writers won't.

8. Enjoy the rush of deadline addiction, but don't let your story dry out and die.

9. Deliver the number of words you promised. If you must pad (with sidebars) or delete, do it. Anticipate, in advance, that worst-case scenario.

10. Before you criticize articles you could write better, see what works for them.

11. Be dependable.

What's Next?

You're ready to connect with an editor. Here's how.

CHAPTER 2

Making Contact

Never buy an editor or publisher a lunch
or a drink until he has bought an article,
story or book from you.

JOHN CREASEY

Unless your manuscript is requested by an editor, you could end up in the slush pile. Think about that word, slush. It's as cold, unappealing and unproductive as it sounds. One New York publisher even has a slush room. Once a month, the editorial assistants are treated to "slunch," where they have an opportunity to eat in, courtesy of the company, and go through that unappealing slush pile. You can guess how many manuscripts get purchased that way.

In publishing, as in most of life, everyone is accountable to someone. It is imperative that you address your submission to a real, live human. If not, you will end up in the slush pile, which is not accountable to anyone.

You can find that contact person in a number of ways, from calling the publishing house and just asking, to researching speakers at writers' conferences. Once you have a name, you have a chance, but just one. If your submission is unprofessional, you could lose that chance, and fast.

Editors don't necessarily read from the top of the pile. We reach in, study an envelope, open it and read, but not very far. It doesn't take much for an editor to decide whether to shove that manuscript into the SASE or keep on reading.

Letterhead

Mention letterhead to a roomful of editors, and you'll get numerous stories, ranging from amusing to unbelievable. What's sad is that behind those stories are writers who have no idea that their letterhead makes them and whatever they're submitting look like a joke.

There's the would-be travel writer whose name I've long forgotten but whose letterhead included a cartoon of a woman with a suitcase in one hand and a notebook in the other. Then there was the qualified but insecure writer who used the letterhead and accompanying business card to list every magazine in which he was ever published, or so it appeared. If your published credits can fill a business card, don't advertise the fact. The relevant publications belong in your letter not on your letterhead.

Let me confess that if I see a squirrel sticker lurking on the outside of the envelope, I will not even open it. I've had too many bad experiences with manuscripts arriving in envelopes bearing squirrel stickers.

An agent friend says, "If there's a squirrel sticker on the outside, there will be a business card with, 'John Doe, Freelance Writer' on it, for sure."

She's right, of course. And in this imaginary submission

from hell, count in parchment paper, script font, a single-spaced manuscript and—bet on it—no SASE.

The hapless squirrel sticker has become my metaphor for how NOT to make contact with an editor. You know better than this, of course, and I include it only because of the questions I receive from other writers. After the first *Rulebook* was published, I received an e-mail from a writer in Bangkok. Why, he asked, did I tell writers not to put the words "Freelance Writer" on their letterhead or business cards? It was a good question, and I realized that I hadn't dwelled on it, because I thought everyone knew.

That act alone won't keep an editor from taking you seriously, but after looking at thousands of submissions in my life, let me tell you that it most definitely is a symptom. First, the very content of your query letter should indicate that you're a freelancer. And be honest. Once you get that label on your letterhead, aren't you tempted to add a tasteful logo, perhaps, or at least that pseudo-watermark of the world available with some software programs? And if that squirrel were holding a quill pen... You see how easy it is to let yourself fall into that trap? Spend your time and creativity on what you place inside that envelope.

Some so-called experts say you should stand out. The easiest and best way to do that is by demonstrating good taste. I like Eaton 25 percent Cotton Fibre Private Stock Laid Paper for laser and inkjet printers. You can find it at any office supply store in your choice of some very basic colors like white, light gray, cream. The paper is heavy, 24-pound weight, which should remind you to keep that query letter to one page. Although there may be exceptions to this rule, I have never seen a query that couldn't be improved by shortening to one page.

My letterhead consists of my name, upper and lower case, a rule, and beneath that, on the other side of the page, my contact information, including my e-mail address. Some writers include a social security number, but I think that's presumptuous and possibly risky.

Now that you're stripped down your format and beefed up your content, you're ready to approach an editor. Here are some of the best methods.

The Referral

You can be referred to an editor in many different ways. You might take a class from a published writer. You may have a friend or relative who knows an editor or has sold to a specific publication. Just ask if he or she would mind your dropping their name. Don't be shy, and if they say they'd rather you not, respect that, too. Most writers like helping others connect.

Follow every lead, even the crazy, unlikely ones. I once sold to an editor I met through the owner of a public-relations firm the magazine employed. While working on another story, I mentioned to the PR person my interest in wineries. She told me that she had another client who was editor of a wine magazine and offered me her phone number on the spot. I chickened out on the phone call, but I did get the assignment.

Make your initial approach in writing. Regardless of the importance of the person referring you, be sure your letter includes these two must-have ingredients for any query letter to any editor: (1) Enough information to show that your idea is right for the magazine; and (2) Enough information to show that you're the writer to pull it off.

If you don't have writing credits, don't bring up the subject. List your life credits instead. Are you a teacher writing about education, a politician writing about politics, a nutritionist writing low-cal recipes?

Even more than credits, the way you write the query letter will determine whether or not you're the person for the job. Try to use the same tone in both the query and the article.

Use your contact's name in the first line.

> Dear Joan Editor,
>
> Bonnie Hearn Hill suggested I contact you regarding my proposed article, "Four Cats are Better than One."

That takes care of the first two points that you should make in the letter. If this were a real letter, you would go on to explain the approach you plan to take. Have you researched cat owners, sent out questionnaires, conducted interviews with vets?

Follow that with your publishing and/or life credits. Don't apologize for being unpublished; don't even mention the fact. Don't compare yourself to a famous writer ("This is an Erma Bombeck-type piece, full of humor.") Please don't tell how much your family and friends love it.

Include a timeframe, preferably a short one. If you would like to look at the article, I could send it to you at once.

The sixth rule of queries is to close on a positive note. Not everyone agrees with me here, and I can only report what ending makes me want to respond in the queries I receive.

> I look forward to hearing from you.

Some says this close is redundant. Don't I know that you want to hear back from me? Sure, but when you close with a personal, "I look forward to hearing from you," I'm more committed than with a strictly business close.

Most queries sound as if a machine wrote them. Don't be afraid to sound like a person, and you may even hear from a person in return.

So here they are, the six rules of query. This is all you really need to include:

1. Your famous contact person.
2. The title of the proposed article.
3. The approach (10 tips/three sources) you plan to take.
4. Your publishing and/or life credits, if appropriate.
5. A timeframe for delivering the completed manuscript, preferably, *at once* or *upon request.*
6. A positive close.

These rules change only slightly, regardless of how you connect with an editor. One of the easiest ways to do that is to refer yourself.

The Self-Referral

You have an idea, and you know where you want to send it. This is what salespeople refer to as a "cold call," and if it can work for department store photographers, it can certainly work for you.

Phone the magazine and ask which editor handles what you want to write. Yes, they really will tell you. Send the query to this person, who is probably going to be an articles editor or editorial assistant. I've used Editor as a generic last name here, but remember, it is essential that you address your letter to a real person.

Since you are being referred by yourself, you need to introduce yourself. Are you familiar with the magazine? Do you like it?

Then say something like:

> Dear Joe Editor,
>
> I read and enjoy your magazine, and am hoping you might be interested in my article, "Five Steps to Container Gardening."

Or:

> Dear Jane Assistant Editor,
>
> I read and enjoy your magazine and hope you will agree that my proposed article, "Low-Cal Flan," will be of interest to your readers.

Don't gush or say that you sleep with the magazine under your pillow. Do, however, make it clear that you're familiar with what it publishes.

The self-referral also works if you've seen a listing in a writers' publication.

> Dear Ms. Editor,
>
> I read your recent market listing for literary profiles in the recent issue of *Writing for Money*, and hope you might be interested in looking at "Howling at the Sun," which focuses on the work of three very different poets who were raised in Central California's San Joaquin Valley.

You can also browse conference brochures. Check which editors are appearing at which conferences. This means that they're in the market. Begin your query with a reference to this.

> Dear Jim Editor,
>
> I understand that you will be appearing at the

Southwest Writers Conference in Albuquerque
this year, and I'm hoping you might be willing to
look at my article, "Guide to the Seamless
Screenplay."

No, you didn't say you were going to be in Albuquerque. You
simply implied it. If you are planning to attend, you could add:
I hope to see you there. Either way, you've gotten the editor's attention with more than the touted canned query letter.

The Internet

Many feel that the Internet is going to change the way books are
sold and made. I hope they're right, and we'd all better hope that
online access will also help bring the archaic practice of article
and short story submission into the current, as well as the next
century.

I like the speed of querying online, and I love the lack of
SASES. Many editors now invite on-line submissions. But how
can you say how wonderful you are in a few short sentences? I'll
address online etiquette in greater length at the end of this
chapter. In the meantime, here are some basics.

- Provide the important information first.

  I am a published writer specializing in travel, and I'm
  hoping the enclosed article on sailing sites on Catalina
  Island might be of interest to your readers.

- Don't attach the article or clips unless the guidelines en-
  courage you to do so.

- When you're sending an e-mail query, be certain this is
  an article worthy of the immediacy. Is it timely? Are you

qualified to write it? Is this the editor's preferred method of contact?

If you get a go, you'll love the speed with which such a query can be accepted, evaluated and in print.

The Writers' Conference

Many, many writers connect with editors at conferences. I've seen a homemaker sell her first essay for $1,500 at a conference. I've seen deals made behind the scenes that metaphorically curled even my hair. I've learned industry gossip, been inspired by success stories. In short, I believe that every serious writer should attend at least one writing conference — not a user and loser Podunk, Calif., conference, but the real thing.

My favorite is the Southwest Writers Conference in Albuquerque, N.M. It's five hundred-plus people, the top editors and agents in the country, and pure energy.

If you don't have the funds to fly to Albuquerque this year, consider something closer to home, but make certain publishing professionals will attend. The last thing you want is a bunch of has-beens and never-weres who want to tell you how they did it while they try to sell you their books nobody else would buy.

Here are some solid guidelines for making your way to and around a conference.

- If possible, attend with a friend. You'll be able to cross-promote each other to the editors you meet.
- If you attend alone, make a friend ASAP. Ask what she/he has written and wants to achieve as a result of attending the conference. Try to connect with someone who's as serious about writing as you are.

- Connect in advance. Study the conference brochure and write to the agents/editors you want to pitch. Enclose a short synopsis of your piece.

- Be brave. Most of these professionals attend because they're looking for writers. Feel free to approach anyone during the social hours and meals. Attend every possible party. But do respect the editor's alone time. Don't bang on her hotel-room door, and don't slide your manuscript under the stall in the rest room. While I'm sure this last affront is an urban myth, I'm including the warning because I hear about it all too often.

- Follow up.

Write to the agents and editors. Say, "I met you at the xyz conference last week and enjoyed talking with you. Enclosed is my article /short story/first three chapters of my novel. I'd appreciate your taking a look at it." Even if you don't have something ready to sell, write notes to those you enjoyed meeting and hearing to increase the chances of their remembering you.

Practice my Rule of Follow Up, which may not be statistically accurate but can keep you from procrastinating. Follow up within twenty-four hours of contact with someone. If not, your chances of ever following up are cut by fifty percent. Wait another twenty-four hours and chop off another fifty percent.

The Perfect-Query Myth

As you already know if you've read this far, everyone who's ever wanted to write is looking for The Secret. To many would-be article writers, The Secret is connected to writing The Perfect

Query. The first night of every class I teach, I ask each one attending what he or she wants to learn in those seven or eight weeks. Most of them tell me that all they need to know is how to write a query letter. They speak as if this skill can unlock the world of publishing.

Numerous writers' books support that myth. The query, they tell you, will help you publish, because the editor can help you slant and develop the story her way. In four short words: *Doesn't work like that.*

Here's what the query letter really does. It slows you down. Contrary to what you might have heard, it's much easier to reject a one-page, well-written letter, than it is to reject a complete manuscript that is almost but not quite there. If at all possible (if the guidelines don't scream "Query First"), try sending your compete article with that effective, not nearly as mysterious, cover letter.

A cover letter is a boiled-down version of your query, without the boring part. Use your usual introduction, depending on whether you've been referred, are referring yourself, are using e-mail or trying to connect with a conference speaker. Then say: *Enclosed is an article I hope you will consider for publication.*

No one is going to faint or think you gauche. Many editors, in spite of what's printed in their guidelines, don't mind looking at the first page or two of your article, and you already know that they won't look at more if the first part doesn't grab them.

Continue with the letter, including your title, credits, if appropriate, and your usual positive close. Tuck in a self-addressed, stamped envelope, just in case the editor doesn't share your affection for the piece. I know this method works; it's worked for me.

In the early nineties, I had an idea for an article that might work for others. I realized that most writers spent their time and energy, as I did, trying to craft a wonderful lead. No one paid any attention to how an article should finish. Many tied it up in a bow, when the ending should really open it up to the reader's emotions and thoughts.

At the time I considered how to end a piece, I was trying, not so successfully, to write my first book, *Focus Your Writing*. Once I started thinking and researching the various ways of ending an article, I knew I wanted to sell this one before the *Focus* book was finished. I longed to query *Writer's Digest*, but I didn't have the nerve to attempt trying to sell to this magazine I had studied since it was truly digest-size.

All right, I thought. I had to write the chapter anyway. Why not write it, then try to sell it as an article? That's how "The Last Word" was submitted to *WD*. I'm convinced a query letter would have been sent back the same day. Instead, I received my manuscript in the mail with a long letter from the articles editor suggesting that I make some changes and include some actual examples.

I made the changes, included the examples, and sold the article. I also used the editor's suggestions (and the *WD* clip) to make *Focus Your Writing* a better book.

The *WD* editor could reject my query, if I'd sent one, but she could see the potential in the article I sent instead. So much for the Perfect-Query Myth. If there's any way you can send the entire article, do so.

The Old-Fashioned Query

In spite of that, many publications still expect and appreciate the old-fashioned query letter. Some get downright nasty about it, returning your manuscript with a form letter instructing you to query first. That sounds too little like a magazine and too much like the IRS.

Again, I think if the magazine is ambiguous regarding its standards for submission, send the entire piece. If you're writing for a newspaper, send the entire piece for sure.

If you must send a query, observe the six rules of query listed earlier in this chapter. Again, you must show why the article will sell, and you must also show them why you're the person to write it. Whether query or cover letter, state your accomplishments without fanfare. If you have published clips (photocopies of articles you've written), include them. If not, go with solid life experience (or nothing) instead of pseudo credits such as sixth honorable mention in a local contest.

In Praise of E-Mail Queries

The worst part about old-fashioned queries are those SASES. Maybe because I know firsthand the sinking, shameful feeling of seeing one of my own SASES peeking out of my mailbox at home, I've always hated having to stuff those piles of paper from other writers back into their pre-stamped envelopes. Now, thanks to the e-mail query, I may no longer have to.

If you're one of the few out there who still doesn't have an e-mail account, I strongly advise you to consider it. Likewise, if your service provides a member profile, use it. One freelancer told me he'd received four paying writing assignments from his profile on America Online.

The number of editors willing to read e-mail queries increases all the time, as well it should. No longer does an editor have plow through a mountain of manuscripts looking for just one that will work. No longer do you have to waste paper and postage only to wait weeks or months for a reply. And if the editor passes on your idea, you won't suffer a major disappointment.

Multiple queries are even easier online. Besides, you won't have to contend with that ill-fated brown envelope exposing itself to you and your spying neighbors. You won't have to look at those wrinkled, coffee-stained pages reeking of failure.

Since just the good ideas make it past the initial e-mail screening, the percentage of queries-per-sale goes up. The editor's desk is covered with possibilities and promise instead of rejections waiting to happen.

If yours is one of the requested manuscripts, you're instantly screened in. If you lack knowledge of e-mail etiquette, however, you'll never make it that far.

"The Internet has given us new tools, but writers need to know how to use those tools," says Doris Booth, who operates Authorlink.com, an online editor-, agent-referral service for writers. In less than two years, she connected more than ninety writers with literary agents as a result of online exposure, and has accomplished much more since then.

Who Are You?

According to Booth, most writers forget to list full contact information on the bottom of e-mail queries.

"Believe it or not, it happens all the time," she said.

You may be HOTMAMA online, but that won't help the editor reading your query. Be sure that you put full contact information on the top or bottom of your e-mail. List Web site information here, if appropriate. Don't just say something like, "Go to my Web site for more about me."

"Editors and agents do not visit individual writers' sites, and they hate it when they're asked to," Booth said.

An e-mail query is similar to a regular query in length. If anything, it should probably be shorter.

> I am a published freelance writer responding to
> your online request for medical writers.

Unless the editor has indicated otherwise, try to pitch one idea at a time. A list of possible topics waters down the impact of each.

Double-check, make that triple-check, your finished letter. Some programs will do this for you. Otherwise, you might want to create a separate document, spell-check it and copy it onto your message. You will be judged on the basis of this one letter.

Make certain that you've spelled the editor's name correctly and gotten the title and the gender right. If you're not sure, "Dear Pat Smith," is perfectly acceptable.

Do not, under any circumstances, attach the article, clips, your bio, a photo of your dog or anything else to the letter unless the guidelines specifically instruct you to do so. This is probably the biggest e-mail violation, and it's just that—a violation of the editor's time. Sitting in front of the terminal while the computer chugs and wheezes to deliver an epic from a stranger will leave the editor with less than charitable feelings about the writer.

With the e-mail query, perhaps more than ever, don't forget that there's a real live person on the other end of the line. Extend to that fellow human the same courtesy and professionalism you would in a snail-mail query. Combine it with a focused, timely idea you are qualified to write, and you'll have a query that almost any editor will be forced to consider—and no SASE.

Quirks That Work

Because I know how business-size envelopes fall off of my free-lance pile at work, I always mail my freelance queries flat, in a white manuscript envelope. I include a business-size SASE *behind* the letter so as not to invite rejection. These are clearly quirks, not rules, but they're quirks that work for me. The Rule of Twelve is another.

Many writers believe in the Rule of Twelve — that is, with twelve manuscripts in the mail, you will sell. I've seen this rule work, often uncannily, with writers in my class, but I remind myself that it also worked for me when I kept ten manuscripts in the mail at all times.

The real rule here, I suspect, is to circulate several projects at once to any number of markets. When you find a receptive editor, you can focus on that market. Until then, the Rule of Twelve or twenty, if that's what it takes, should serve you well. When you do finally connect, the next chapter may come in handy.

Exception to the Rule: The Human Element

Picture an editor, any editor, any publication. We are not machines. We are people with jobs we may or may not enjoy. You can help make those jobs easier for us. That's what we're hoping when we open that envelope from you.

The worst submissions I receive are the careless, photo-copied articles with form cover letters, and sometimes no cover letter at all. On the other hand, the clever, by-the-book Perfect Queries are almost as impersonal.

I believe the human approach is best. Learn the editor's name and use it. *Dear Ms. Hill* or even *Dear Bonnie Hill.* If you should talk to the editor on the phone, know before you call, what you want to happen as the result of the conversation. Don't wander, and keep in mind what the editor may want from this conversation too. It can vary from getting off of the phone to meet a deadline to finding someone to cover a piece on rodeo clowns or financial planning for children.

I met one of my all-time very best editors in 1997. Our first conversation symbolized the kind of working and personal relationship that followed. Of course, I had no way of predicting that when my phone rang early one morning, and a pleasant-sounding young woman told me she was the new editor and had been pleased with the reader response to a recent article about me her magazine had published.

All I could think about as I listened was: *She wants to offer me an assignment.* I wasn't thinking about her or her needs, just that this was an Editor, capital E, and I just might get something out of it.

As a result, I was almost speechless with shock when she did not offer me an assignment but instead said, "We'd like you to be a columnist for us."

Her decency sort of shocked me back to reality. This human was offering me something greater than I'd dared to imagine. Finally I was able to get out of my own head and think about her. I don't know where the words came from, but I actually heard myself ask, "And what are your personal goals? What would you like to see happen with the magazine?"

I still can't believe I dared to get that personal on a first phone call, but in this case, I didn't have time to think about it. Before I could hang up and shoot myself, she answered with the same candor, about her goals and herself.

In a few weeks, she was giving me choice assignments along with my column. I knew the name of her husband and her cats. I learned more about writing by watching what she left out and changed in my articles. As my professional respect grew, so did our friendship. I've often wondered if we'd ever have become this close if I had restrained myself during that first conversation about *me*, when I instead blundered in without invitation and started asking about *her*.

Not everyone is lucky enough to find a soul mate when seeking an editor, of course. If you want more than one sale to the magazine, however, you'll need to build a relationship with the editor. Don't fake it, but if you feel it, treat this person *as* a person. Ask an occasional question, and always study the changes the editor made to your article. Don't worry about what you really meant when you wrote it. Try to figure out what the editor wanted, and if you're uncomfortable (not defensive) about the changes, just ask.

Again, please forget the Perfect Query Myth. Write to your editor as one human to another, not as the guy tap-dancing across her desk, trying to dazzle her with his footwork. Don't just write to that editor. Reach her.

The Next Eight Rules

12. Address everything you submit to a real human not to "Editor."

13. Don't get too creative with your letterhead. Save that for what you write beneath it.

14. Avoid squirrel stickers and parchment paper, and seriously consider if you want to refer to yourself as *Jane Doe, Freelance Writer* on your business card.

15. Connect with an editor through a referral, a self-referral, Internet query, writers' conference, and don't believe the Perfect Query Myth.

16. Practice the six rules of query.

17. Send the manuscript, and not the query, whenever possible.

18. Practice the quirky Rule of Twelve or your own quirky rule. Just keep many manuscripts in the mail at all times.

19. Approach editors as human first. Most of us are.

What's Next?

You're a freelancer. You may have already landed an assignment. It's time to follow through and deliver.

CHAPTER 3

Following Through

A deadline is negative inspiration.
Still it's better than no inspiration at all.

RITA MAE BROWN

Little in a writer's life equals that day when the mail arrives or the telephone rings, bringing an assignment from an editor. You want to throw a party, call everyone who ever loved you, to scream to the world, "I did it."

Directly upon the heels of that joy, steps the realization that you're actually going to have to write this thing you've proposed. Can you do it and do it well? Can you deliver it on time?

These little insecurities never really seem to go away. We sell that first article, and the second gets a little easier. Even by the fifteenth or the five thousandth, we still ride that teeter-totter of joy and fear. That may even be part of what makes us good and keeps us on our toes. In spite of past success, we don't take the future for granted. If we did, we might get sloppy.

Of course, if you wrote the article first, you're staring only a rewrite in the face, not a ream of blank paper. Ultimately, you will begin receiving assignments, either because of a query letter you've submitted or because the editor liked your last piece. Here's how to give that editor what s/he expects.

Start Your Assignment When It's Assigned.

Your editor will be less than thrilled if you call the day before deadline to explain that you couldn't reach your sources. If you'd started the assignment the month before, you could have communicated your problem much sooner, thus giving the editor a more reasonable chance to come up with other possibilities for all of those blank pages that have been assigned to you.

Don't assume the source will be ready at the last minute just because you are. If time is tight, call ahead and arrange a telephone interview in advance. That's what I had to do when I was working on a book and an article, with deadlines two days apart. For the article, I had to interview the editors of *Time, Newsweek* and *U.S. News.*

My initial encounter at each publication was with a communications director who screened my call, determined what information I required, sent and faxed me the required facts and supporting articles and scheduled the interviews so that I could plug in fresh quotes. All three telephone interviews took place that Saturday night and Sunday morning, and I e-mailed the article to my editor the following Monday.

Deadlines this tight will prove to you that you really are a writer. Any deadline, however, will arrive far too soon if you don't plan for it.

Understand, in Advance, about Sources.

This is easy. When you get the assignment, ask the editor, "Do you have contacts you'd like me to include, or do you prefer that

I use my own sources?"

Many editors know exactly whom they want you to contact. Others don't have a clue. Once you know what's expected, you'll have a better idea of how to plan your time.

You should always include a list of your sources and contact information as the last page of your manuscript. Some magazines require this. Others just have fact-checkers who appreciate it.

Consider Telephone Interviews.

The telephone interview saves time for both you and your subject. It makes it possible for you to relax at the kitchen table and juggle your notes without worrying how you look.

Of course, the ideal interview would allow you to see the person you're addressing, to describe his environment and mannerisms, the way he or she reacts to your questions. Even if you live close enough to do this, you can still complete most of the interview on the phone. Just tell the subject you need some background information before the person-to-person interview.

Take Notes as Direct Quotes.

I can't tell you how irritating it is to receive a so-called interview from a writer whose notes were too sketchy to include direct quotes. You'd be surprised how many published writers consider partial quotes good enough. An example: *Jones said the décor trend for spring will be "bright and comfortable," with touches of "sophisticated elegance."*

That's not what Jones said. It's only the part you jotted down. You could be attributing sentiments to your subject that don't actually exist, and that's about as bad as it gets. Write down the answers to your questions as direct quotes whenever possible. This will provide you with more options later when you decide what to paraphrase and what to quote directly in your finished article.

Write as You Go.

Finish your interview, hang up the telephone, and write—right now—while it's still fresh. Create a working title and lead and plug in facts and quotes as you go. This way you'll see where the holes are, and you won't have to sit down the night before deadline with a stack of scrawled notes.

"But I do better under pressure," you say. So do I, and so do any number of masochists. But we aren't writing for the rush of adrenaline; we're writing for the person on the other end. There's an editor depending on you to deliver. Don't set yourself up for failure.

Copy the Format.

Organize and format your story so that it looks like everything else the magazine prints. Some publications use short, punchy titles followed by subheads. Others use long titles. By studying the publication, you can determine which, and you can provide the same.

As you are well aware, editors are busy. Picture this person on deadline, trying to fit a jumble of words into the available pages. Along comes your manuscript, complete with appropriate subheads and suggested sidebars. I've had editors practically promise to name their next child after me for supplying something as simple as a subhead.

On the converse side, don't try to reinvent the magazine, no matter how sincere your intentions. The worst thing you can do is suggest improvements to an editor, especially in the area of format.

If the Editor Asks for a Rewrite, Comply. Nicely.

This probably won't happen if you've been communicating, but sometimes the editor may decide the article should be longer or that an additional source needs to be included, or, at worst, that the article needs a major overhaul.

One of my colleagues rewrote an essay bemoaning family budgets for a national women's magazine because the editorial board, not the editor, felt the tone made the writer sound spoiled. After one rewrite, the article was accepted.

I've also heard the story about numerous writers who lost assignments and contracts because they wouldn't change a word.

Ask Enough Questions.

It's your responsibility to make sure that you understand what the editor expects. If you frequently are asked to rewrite, you're not communicating, and the relationship will probably not last very long.

Ask for Feedback.

An editor who's already purchased from you will be more likely to tell you what did and didn't work as well as share likes and dislikes. Most editors do not comment on less-than-perfect manuscripts, for two very good reasons. (1) Either, the writer becomes your new best friend and calls to say the revise "you requested" is in the mail, and you will publish it now, won't you? Or (2) the writer calls to say you're a jerk, with no idea what

Ten Classic Crashes

Herewith are the ten all-time worst excuses for missing a deadline.

1. *My computer crashed.* You can't believe how many times we editors hear this.

2. *My car crashed (and on the way to mail this, at that).* It could happen, but if you'd been serious about delivering the article, would you have waited until the last minute to turn it in?

3. *My contact crashed.* You're so cool that you didn't even try for the interview until one day before deadline. Now you find out that your big source is spending the month in Jamaica. If this were a TV game show, you'd be hearing a big buzz right now.

4. *The cat crashed (and woke up shredding the story).* Sure, and the dog ate your homework. One writer (I swear) actually claimed that his bird pecked the article to shreds while trying to make a nest. Even if it's true, don't embarrass yourself by repeating the story. Stay up all night if you must, and write another one.

5. *My grandmother crashed (and she's never getting up).* I know one editor who got that funeral excuse three times — from the same writer.

6. *My wrists crashed.* You'd think carpal tunnel syndrome was approaching epidemic proportions. This excuse has now eclipsed the flu as the most common deadline illness.

7. *My Rolodex crashed.* Telling the editor that you lost her address is not a suitable explanation for missing a deadline.

8. *My Federal Express delivery crashed.* I can count on half a hand the number of times I've had to trace a lost Fed Ex package.

9. *My priorities crashed.* One of my editors told me she was called, on deadline day, no less, by a seasoned freelancer. He told her he was "just swamped," with other jobs which, "frankly pay me more." He expected her to be pleased that she would receive the story by the end of the week.

10. *I crashed.* This isn't the sixties. Your allergies, breakdowns and drug busts are no excuse to miss a deadline. Keep your personal problems personal. Just meet your commitments.

constitutes good writing, and you'd better look both ways, baby, before leaving your office tonight. If an editor gives you feedback, don't resist. Say, "Thank you."

Let the Editor Know You're Available.

A short e-mail or written note when the article appears is also appreciated. Don't be shy about querying an editor who has bought from you.

Unless the editor has indicated otherwise, try to pitch one query at a time. A list of possible topics waters down the impact of each. The editor decides to look at it later, because it's too complex for an immediate decision.

Let It Simmer.

Once you finish the article, resist the impulse to rush to the nearest post office. That manuscript you wrote in the heat of passion is now ready for a cold editorial eye. Yours. Take your time and sit on the piece for a while. You'll be amazed what you discover when you come back to it after a few days.

The Rules of Follow-Through

20. Start your article when it's assigned, even if the deadline is far in the future.

21. Don't assume the source will be available at the last minute.

22. Determine in advance if you should find your own sources.

23. Also inquire about length and focus of the piece.

24. Investigate the possibility of finding sources online.

25. Although the Internet is fine for research, don't mistake an online chat for an interview.

26. Include a list of sources and contact information with the manuscript.

27. Conduct a telephone interview.

28. Take notes as direct quotes.

29. Write as you go, from the first interview on.

30. Copy the publication's format, right down to the subheads.

31. If possible, give your story time to simmer.

32. If asked for a rewrite, comply.

33. If you disagree with the editing job, don't expect it to improve with future articles. Move on to another editor, another publication.

34. Invite but don't expect feedback.

35. Let the editor know that you're available for future assignments.

What's Next

Next, we'll look at a subject many writers are convinced they don't need—revision.

CHAPTER 4

Vision & Revision

Work is so much more fun than fun.

NOEL COWARD

Little in a writer's life is more empowering than sitting down at the computer or its equivalent and watching your words fill the screen. Conversely, little is more humbling than sitting down at the computer, the kitchen table or the equivalent, and trying to revise those words.

That masterpiece in your mind seldom makes it to the page intact. Revision provides the second chance to get it right and the last chance to spot what's wrong before the editor steps in.

After working as an editor for more than ten years, I briefly considered writing a book on revision. "Don't be crazy," an agent friend said. "No one would buy it. They don't think they need to revise."

She went on to tell me that a major publisher of books for writers had let its revision title go out of print. To the agent, I said yes, that it was not a great idea, after all. To myself, I said: *Damn. What do you mean they don't need to revise?*

I have yet to meet a writer who didn't need just that. They do. I do, and so do you.

Time Is Not on Your Side

Along with the less-than-happy news that your article may need more time for editing, is the reality that you probably have written up to deadline, either an imposed one or one of your own making. In a more perfect world, we could be like Archibald MacLeish, who said he put his poems in a drawer, to either ripen or rot, like apples. In order to determine the condition of his metaphorical apples, MacLeish knew he needed some space between him and them.

Most of us have little ripening time between final draft and deadline. If possible, try to give yourself twenty-four hours from when you think you've finished until the final edit. Even better, and if time allows, give the manuscript to a writing friend (not a spouse or non-writing family member) and offer to return the favor.

And If You Don't Have Time?

Then you have to do it yourself, and you'll need some rules.

Just because you're revising your manuscript doesn't mean you have to trash it. Start with the story you wanted to tell. Is it there on the page? If not, what's missing? Now, look at what you meant to say when you wrote it, the subtext. This is a story about what? Your last three jobs? But what's the subtext? What's it really about? The ability to reinvent ourselves? The way we fool ourselves by cloaking our patterns in the language of change? Identify story and subtext. Your first edit shouldn't be tainted with judgment. It should address only focus and clarity. Do you have a promise, proof and payoff for the reader? Is it clear from the title and lead what you intend to tell the reader?

Next, do a line edit. Read your piece sentence by sentence, word by word. The goal is to look at it without editorial ownership, or as Faulkner instructed, to "kill your darlings." Kill you must. Like most writers, you probably experience difficulty spotting, let alone killing, the darlings in your article.

Start by reading your manuscript aloud, pen in hand. Make a check mark by every word or phrase you especially love. Then, consider getting rid of it, unless it really contributes to the purpose of the piece. Most of the ones you love exist for some reason beyond their importance to the article you're writing.

You've always relied on *etc.,* and those mountains were truly *beautiful.* Or did you just opt for the easiest word? Don't let these bad habits substitute for what you really mean. Take *etc.* If the chef prepared pan-braised salmon, kale and a salad of baby greens, etc., complete the thought. Was it served with a hazelnut dressing? Then, say so. *Etc.* means that you ran out of items, maybe because the items you listed were enough. Effective writing involves selection.

No one can visualize *beautiful.* The careful writer paints a more specific picture for the reader. One person's beautiful retreat is another's barren desert. That's what's wrong with nonspecific words like *beautiful.* They aren't specific enough.

The superlatives (*He was the greatest writer of the twentieth century*) aren't backed by anything, and we doubt the best, the smartest, the most beautiful and any other superlatives that the loose talkers try to shove into our lives.

Rule: If you can use it to describe three unrelated subjects, it's probably not specific enough to communicate your meaning. Think: Beautiful mountains; beautiful girl, beautiful dog. Not very specific, is it? And we haven't even touched upon beautiful dinner.

Try this same exercise with *lovely*. Lovely mountains; lovely girl; lovely dog, lovely dinner, thank you very much.

Let's try, *interesting*. The mountains, the girl, the dog and the dinner don't pass, do they?

I had a student whose wife passively put him down when, after looking at one of his stories, she smiled and said, "That's very interesting." We'll talk more about sabotage in Chapter 9. For now, it's enough to remember that a nonspecific word can connote any number of meanings.

While you're congratulating yourself on the darlings you've already detected, take an honest look at what might be the biggest darling of all—your first paragraph. You wrote it to launch your piece, thus it appears to belong there. Perhaps your article grew in an entirely different direction. Is that lead now a true start or a false start?

New Discoveries

You're so impressed with that new word you've just learned that you have to flaunt it, right now. Words float in and out of vogue on a regular basis. All of a sudden, I'll see dozens of freelance manuscripts peppered with *ubiquitous, myriad,* and more recently, *eponymous,* an adjective that, in its simplest form, means *named after.* As in, Joe's eponymous restaurant.

As you're falling in love with these words, so is every other well-read writer on the planet. Ask yourself if the word really adds to your piece, or if it is a self-conscious darling.

I-Strain

That anecdote from your childhood is the perfect lead for your piece on making apricot jam. Maybe so, but you could be suffering what is sometimes referred to as I-strain. Writers love writing about themselves. Their favorite word is, "I," yet the reader's favorite word is, "You." Ad copywriters probably know this better than anyone. Not, "We're having a sale," but "You can save."

Your first-person anecdote might fit in a column, an essay or a personal-experience piece. Does it really enhance your article, or is it an exercise in terminal I-strain?

Orphan Quotes

It was "love at first sight," when you visited the restaurant, especially when you sampled that tray of assorted "munchies." Okay. So the words within those quotation marks were never spoken by any human. You know that, but quote marks are just kind of "cute," aren't they?

Afraid not. Editors recognize them, on sight, as orphan quotes, which draw attention to weak writing. Only a quotation that can be attributed to a speaker can be set off with quotation marks. Send those orphans back to the orphanage and come up with a fresh word or phrase that says what you mean.

Writers who rely on these insidious little darlings will fight to the death before they give them up. "But I call my cats my furry kids," one of my students said, making scary quote marks with her fingers in the air.

Why does she need quotes, when her meaning is clear and specific?

Some go as far as slamming in a single orphan quote, to signal, I suppose, that this isn't a legitimate, quoted statement, you're reading here, folks.

Even in this abbreviated garb, it's still an orphan. Just as double quotes exist for a reason (to quote a human who actually spoke the words), single quotes exist for a reason (to quote a human quoting a human who actually spoke the words). Here's an example.

> Matt told me she was rude once they got to the
> party. "She didn't bother beating around the
> bush," he told me. "Just before she got out of the
> car, she said, 'Thanks for the ride, creep. Now,
> get lost.'"

Punctuation Crutches

When you sense your language hobbling along, trailing off, you slap in one of these darlings an exclamation point! A colon or semi-colon; or better yet, the ubiquitous ellipses... I probably don't have to remind you that this fondness of excess again usually signals weak prose.

F. Scott Fitzgerald said an exclamation point is like laughing at your own joke. Students who have grown dependent on them are sometimes uncomfortable letting them go. They come up with examples, arguing, "Well, wouldn't an exclamation point work better here than a period?"

Maybe so, but they seldom appear alone. The problem with these babies is that they tend to run in packs. Tell me how many times you've used just one dot-dot-dot, just one exclamation point? Show me one, and I'll bet I can show you a whole colony.

Colons and semi-colons add a scholarly tone that may sound archaic in a consumer article. They also blend sentences and slow your pace. Examine each one with a judicious eye.

Thanks to certain word-processing grammar-checkers, I now see semicolons everywhere, even in dialogue. This is especially jarring. How could the person quoting hope to know whether or not the subject mentally inserted a semicolon in the middle of his statement? It stops the reader cold.

Ellipses do not substitute for dashes or periods. They're meant to indicate missing words from a quotation. Too many probably indicate that you're counting on punctuation to prop up your writing. Even properly used, you need only three (or four, if it's at the end of the sentence, and the fourth is really a period).

Common Editing Errors

After editing as many manuscripts as I have, one starts knowing where to look for problems. It's helpful for you to know what most writers do wrong, so that you can look for these common errors in your own manuscripts.

Most common is *your* used instead of *you're* to mean *you are*. Equally abused is *it's* as a possessive. *Its* never takes an apostrophe unless you're using it as the contraction for *it is*. I'm almost embarrassed mentioning this to professional writers, but too many of us still need reminding. Computer spell-check programs seem to have worsened the problem, perhaps because they too haven't figured out the difference between *there*, the place, and *their*, belonging to them, or *led* through the door and *lead* in a pencil. I continue to see writers who use *peak* when they mean *pique* (as in pique your interest) and *till* instead of *'til*, or better yet, *until*.

Before you use the computer spell-check, go over the manuscript yourself and see how many of these common errors you can spot.

Have you used the right word the right way? If you mean *eager,* don't say *anxious.* If you're talking about distance, it's *farther,* not *further.* Do you know that *preventative* is a noun, and that you need *preventive* if you're writing about a preventive measure? Have you stayed away from trendy slang ("Pushing the envelope," "crunching numbers," "I don't want to go there" "This isn't brain surgery") and non-words like *firstly, secondly, lastly* and *most importantly?*

Make certain your verbs are true verbs, not recycled nouns. You've probably seen or heard the results of such creativity gone amok on television or in the business world, which seems to favor any phrase, however ridiculous, that sounds new. Such verbing of nouns sounds new all right, and it leaves us with sentences like, "I'll pencil you in," or this one I recently received in a press release from a builder. "The development grand opens on Saturday." Can't you almost hear that chalk on the blackboard?

Have you avoided jargon and capitalized only proper nouns? Most editors today prefer fewer capitalized words. Our language suffers, to a certain extent, from what we do for a living. Many journalists I know are jargon junkies. We can't help it. That's what working in a hurry-up, deadline-based business has done to the way we communicate.

Other professions create cap-happy writers. Give me a lawyer, a teacher or someone with a military background, and it's cap city. If you work in one of these fields pay extra attention to the frequency of capitals in your prose.

Have you reworked passive constructions? Check for: *There are, there is, there was* sentences. Find what's really happening in the sentence. There was too much garlic in the gazpacho. There was a single hotel on the Mexican beach. Verbs are power, and these sentences are verb-poor. Skip right over the *was* words and make the garlic or the hotel the subject of your sentence. Too much garlic (verb) the gazpacho. A single hotel (verb) on the Mexican beach. Remember that *was* words also travel in packs. A few won't hurt your piece, but chances are that if you find one, you'll find more.

Have you yanked out excessive adverbs and adjectives? Be especially suspicious of the double "It was a dark and stormy night," variety. One adjective is bad enough. Doubling up in such a manner only weakens each one.

Have you varied the lengths of your sentences? Circle every *And* or *But* that starts a sentence. Too many of these will kill your pace and give a long-winded quality to the piece.

Have you followed the style of the publication? If you're writing in AP Style, do you know that all ages (whether 6, 10 or 99) are written as numerals, as are percentages, such as 3 *percent?* Do you know if the editor prefers *said* or *says?* How does the publication refer to sources in the second reference? Is Mary Jones referred to as *Jones,* she would be in AP Style, or is she *Mary,* as she might be in many women's magazines?

Exceptions to the Rules

None of this means you have to write a paint-by-number piece. It just means that you should be aware of the rules and be sure you have good reason to break them. If you're careless, thinking you'll let the editor make the final call, you may be in for a surprise. That's going to be your byline on the article, not the editor's. Do everything you can to make yourself proud of that article that will carry your name.

It happens. Some editors let mistakes slip past and fail to improve a piece; others make it worse. I was shocked to discover that an editor for a writers' magazine loaded one of my articles with exclamation points and orphan quotes. I couldn't use the article for a clip, although I did share it with my students, who had a good laugh at my expense. The experience reminded me that not all editors are perfect. Indeed, some are so clumsy and/or disrespectful of the writers' voice that they leave their fingerprints all over the manuscript.

You can't control what happens to that piece after you submit it, although you can pass, as I did, on a second chance to work with an editor who butchers your prose. Your only chance of surviving poor or mediocre editing is to edit yourself and be sure your copy is as clean as possible when you submit it. A good editor will appreciate your efforts, and a not-so-good one will have less chance of making you look bad.

It's not that you can't have ellipses, an exclamation mark or an extra-long sentence once in a while. Just be aware of how often you do. Not every editor is going to catch every mistake, and the revision you do on your own will give you a stronger piece in print.

How Do You Sound?

Don't forget to do a final read-through for tone. After all that editing, do you still sound like you? If it's a humorous piece, can you tell that from the first paragraph? If it's an essay, is your voice clear from the start? If your attitude shows up in the piece, is it woven throughout and not stuck on at the end? Is your tone suitable to the tone of the publication?

Finally, have you respected your reader? Have you been too cute, coy or gushy? Have you talked down? If so, remember these words from Jack Bickham: "Don't write down to your readers; the ones dumber than you can't read."

You wouldn't scribble a few notes and send them off to your editor. Don't send a manuscript you haven't revised. Revision isn't all that difficult, and it's an important tool that allows you to narrow the space between that original vision in your head and what you actually wrote.

The Rules of Revision

36. Understand that everyone needs revision.

37. If possible, put some time between you and the finished manuscript.

38. Kill your literary darlings.

39. Think *you,* not *me.*

40. Omit *etc.,* unspecific language, and seriously consider the effectiveness of your lead.

41. Avoid trendy words or terms.

42. Learn and avoid common editing errors.

43. Eliminate orphan quotes.

44. Also eliminate excessive exclamation points, colons, semicolons, ellipses.

45. Remember that no punctuation mark is wrong all of the time. However, if you see yourself repeating one mark or sliding into one style; this is the time to consider how much the mark/style may limit you.

46. Avoid using too many capital letters.

47. Don't be a jargon junkie.

48. Rework passive constructions.

49. Yank most adjectives and adverbs.

50. Vary the lengths of your sentences.

51. Follow the style of the publication.

52. Learn the rules of grammar, but don't take this accomplishment too seriously.

What's Next?

Now that you know how to write and submit, there's something else you must learn, and it's just as difficult as the rest. In the next chapter, we'll talk about how to wait.

CHAPTER 5

Winning the Waiting Game

Don't count the days.
Make the days count.

MUHAMMAD ALI

The late Gary Provost, a fine author and teacher, had this observation of how writers learn of a sale. "Bad news arrives in the mail," Provost said. "Good news comes on the phone." Most of my good news has come in that way, and pretty rapidly at that.

Conversely, I, like other writers, could bore you with the story of the check in the SASE I almost threw away. My guess is that with e-mail simplifying our lives, good news, and bad, will find us sooner.

Although the mailbox holds an occasional surprise, Provost's law holds true most of the time. What happens between the submission and the ultimate response is what many of us call the Waiting Game, and it can make you crazy.

Here's what usually happens when an editor receives a

query or article submission. First, she or he scans the first paragraph or two. Then s/he mentally scrolls down to the writer's credits. Most articles—ninety-eight percent or so—miss the mark, because (1) The writer hasn't researched the publication's needs, or (2) The writing isn't up to par.

The "X" Factor

Many articles are simply too ordinary. They contain no interesting slant; they lack freshness. Why would I buy a freelance piece on how to make candy when I can buy a package of recipes from a syndicate? Does this mean your candy article won't fly? Not unless you find a different slant. The right editor might consider an article on how to make candy from geranium petals, or how a famous person makes candy or how to duplicate the best of See's and Godiva chocolates without the price.

An editor is looking for the "X" factor, that special something only the right writer can provide. Out of a hundred or more submissions, we might find one or two that fit our needs. The Yes letters or phone calls go out at once, as do the No-thanks rejection letters. Those that are not an easy Yes or an easy No go into the Maybe pile.

The Dreaded Piles

That's right. While you're rushing to the mailbox or pouncing on the telephone each time it rings, your poor, once-timely article could be languishing in some editor's Maybe pile, probably after languishing in the Slush pile. The worst thing about that Maybe pile is that it's usually really a No pile traveling incognito.

An even worse fate is the New Writers with Potential pile, which the editor has every intention of getting to—when she has time to individually develop the two thousand-plus writers who have demonstrated a spark of potential.

A scary thought, isn't it? The editor likes your idea too much to reject it outright. He/she places it in that big, fat pile to be considered in some far-off future. And there's nothing you can do—or is there?

Find Out Where You Stand

You have every right to inquire as to the status of your article or query. What's the worst-case scenario? Let me guess. After six weeks or sixteen, you write to the editor, inquiring about your manuscript. He/she digs through the Maybe pile and knows on sight that there is no way in this century it's going to be purchased.

Thus, you receive a rejection, not because you asked, and certainly not because you angered the editor. Your inquiry simply hastened the rejection process, which is not the worst fate, because at least, like it or not, you know, and you can check that market off your list.

One magazine editor told me that he had never published one article from his Maybe pile. My odds are a little better, but not much. Exceptions do occur, however. Editors change jobs. Manuscripts get misplaced. Occasionally, an article or book will take a little while to click.

One of my students sold to the first publication to which he had submitted his piece—more than one year later. The publication had moved, and his manuscript had literally fallen through the cracks. The writer had continued submitting and had received forty-two rejections before he received the call from his dream market of two million readers.

He might have inquired, and so should you. This is not a

bank loan for which you've applied. It's a worthwhile product in search of a buyer. If you don't take action, you may never hear.

I sent a query to someone in 1994, before I sold my first book. Although I should know better, I seldom do when it comes to my own work. I kept finding reasons to prolong the day I would have to check back with this person who probably hated my book. While I was procrastinating, the book sold. I dutifully notified everyone to whom I had submitted it, except the silent editor, who clearly didn't care. She has yet to return my SASE.

Did she lose the manuscript, perhaps? Did she hate it so much that she steamed off the stamps and tossed the rest in the trash? I will never know, because I lacked the courage to do what you must, and that is face the possibility of rejection. You do this by taking a proactive stance.

The Follow-up Letter

Check the reference publication where you found the market listing in the first place. How long before you can expect a response? Note it on your calendar. When the day passes (but not before), query the query. Write a letter, with SASE, of course, to the editor.

Say: *I am writing to inquire as to the status of my article, "Editors are Lazy," which I submitted to you June 1. I hope you like the piece, and I look forward to hearing from you.*

Unless the editor has asked you to phone or use e-mail, stick to written communication. The majority of editors prefer snail mail queries and submissions to telephone calls because such submissions allow them to better manage their time.

Texas agent Jean Price, of the Kirkland Literary Agency, once called the publishing process, "getting paid to wait."

I've always liked that definition. This is a business where patience counts, but not passive patience. Sometimes the big sale, the big deal, the big publication happens even faster than the small one. That's not your concern. Your concern is to produce the product, as we say at the newspaper, and let the decimals and zeroes fall where they may.

When I gave this advice to a new writer planning to attend her first writers' conference, she said, "That sounds great, but what exactly is the product?"

To her, the writing was her heart and soul. That's what my writing is to me, and what your writing must be for you, *while it's still in the writing stage.* Anything less won't continually summon us to the computer like the manic fools that we must be in order to finish anything.

Once a piece is written, edited and in the marketing stage, it's the product, a good one, I hope, but a product nonetheless. If it continues to be all that it was in the creation stage, I won't be able to let go of it. I have to send it into the world. I have to move onto the next project, knowing that rejection is part of this game, but not dwelling on that. One of the best ways of ignoring the reality of rejection is to have more than one target market.

The Multiple-Submission Myth

This must be the all-time, most-often-repeated, bald-faced lie in the business. No, editors do not pass around a secret list of writers who had the nerve and self-esteem to submit to more than one publisher at a time. Yes, everyone except the people who write the how-to books (and I'm not so sure about them) send out multiple submissions all the time. You won't live enough years to wait for each editor's response to each idea.

Finally, it's none of the editor's business how you market

your work. Indicating that it's a multiple submission won't make the editor respond in a more timely manner; in fact, quite the opposite might occur. Put yourself in that editor's place. Unless it's the article of the century, are you going to seriously consider something that someone else may have already purchased?

If it's a good idea, the editor owes it to his or her job to respond as rapidly as possible. The editor who acts fastest wins. What is so horrible about that? You look at a new car and tell the dealer that you will let him know. Would you really be surprised if he sold that car to a more eager buyer? You try on a few pairs of shoes, and unable to decide, leave the store. When you return the following weekend, those purple-suede platform boots you'd been thinking about for days are gone. Do you hate the salesperson, or do you think that perhaps you should have acted sooner?

The car dealer, the shoe seller, don't owe you any explanations when someone comes in with the price of the product. As a professional writer, you should treat your potential buyers/editors with a little more respect. Not only is it the best way to do business, but it might help you sell second rights to the article to one of your other original target markets.

The Cat-Canary Letter

Sooner or later, the welcome telephone call or letter will arrive. Once that happens, you need to notify the other editors, just in case that equally mythic "What if they both want my article?" takes place.

You'll feel like the cat grinning through the last canary feather, but don't let your gloating self-love transfer into what may not be your last contact with these potential customers.

Write: *Since submitting my article, "Editors are Lazy," to you in June, I have sold it to another publication and am withdrawing it from consideration. Thank you for looking at it. If you're interested in reprint rights, I'd love to hear from you.*

Using this approach, one of my students sold her first article to two different publications.

Play Nice

It goes without saying that you should conduct yourself professionally, even if you encounter the occasional rude editor. I've never understood writers who keep hounding unprofessional editors about manuscripts submitted years before. If the second attempt at a response doesn't work, the editor is either overwhelmed with a sea of slush, or, face it, unprofessional. Whatever the reason, purchasing and responding to freelance requests are not a priority with this person.

Just write your cat-canary letter and forget this publication until the changing of editors occurs, as it always does with even the most solid of publications.

Writing well is the best revenge. If the piece is good, you will sell it, and you'll get your revenge when you politely notify the editor of that fact. Burning bridges in this business will come back when you least expect it. Every writer I know has a story about a one-time loser who returned as a boss.

While You're Waiting

Start working on your next query for your next article, or if you write essays that don't require queries, let yourself enjoy a little creative time with something you can write and submit while you wait. You might find yourself loving this new project even more than the one you're circulating.

Don't forget exploring reprint and resale markets for your soon-to-be sold article. This waiting period is the best time to consider other possible slants. Looking into reprint markets also gives you a "B" list in case your first submissions should fail. It can also help you turn up reliable markets for other articles.

I once developed a reprint market that paid me only $25 per article. This market, however, bought everything I sent. It was like playing a little slot machine. I'd stick in a postage stamp and take out $25. The slot machine would say, "Thank you. Here's your money, and here are some clips, in case you want to sell this one more time."

All of these tips won't keep you from wondering and worrying, not to mention fantasizing about your dream market. Just keep busy while you're fantasizing, and don't count on anything in this business. Hope is healthy, but desperation is destructive to you and your writing.

You can't control what's going to happen, but you'll feel more in control if you continue your proactive behavior. I've heard that, in order to publish, a writer must have talent, luck and persistence. And if the writer has persistence, s/he needs only one of the other two. Keeping track of your submissions and keeping many in the mail will keep you persistent, and it will also increase your odds of acceptance. In all honesty, you may never learn to like the Waiting Game. What sane human would like going day to day, pretending that the world won't change the moment the telephone rings? You don't have to like it, but by moving forward, you can learn to play it, and to win it as well.

The Rules of Waiting

53. Check your mailbox and open every letter, especially the ones that don't look as if they contain money.

54. Try to include the "X" factor in anything you write.

55. When you don't hear back, find out where you stand.

56. Write a follow-up letter and use snail mail to deliver it.

57. Once it's written, treat your brainchild like a product.

58. Practice multiple submission, and don't even consider another approach.

59. When you sell your piece, notify other markets you previously queried.

60. Conduct your queries and notifications of sales professionally, whether or not the editor deserves it.

61. Start working on your next project.

62. Consider reprint markets for your current project.

63. Remain proactive and persistent, if only because you'll feel better about yourself and about this career you've chosen.

What's Next?

Sooner or later, somebody has to get paid. Since you're the writer, why not you? Learn how to request payment, negotiate payment, and if you must, collect.

CHAPTER 6

The Business of Writing

The two most beautiful words
in the English language are "check enclosed."

DOROTHY PARKER

Contrary to what you may have experienced this far in your career, writing really is a business, and yes, they do give you money for it. At least that's the way it's supposed to work. Of course when you get your first assignment, you want to gush, "I'd do this free."

I felt the same way. Indeed, I hesitated to bring up the subject of money when I was starting. This was as much a reflection of my lack of self-esteem as it was my lack of experience. In my first few years of freelancing, I was hired for a series of medical articles for a group of doctors and an annual report for a local manufacturing company. I had already sold a few pieces, but I didn't even know that I was expected to negotiate. The medical group wanted to pay me by the hour instead of the project (almost always a danger sign). The group's public relations person suggested a low hourly rate with a guarantee of twenty hours a week. I was honest and reported how many hours I worked—never more than five hours a week. Why didn't I complain? I don't know. I'm not the same person today.

At the manufacturing firm, I met with the personnel director, studied materials, worked diligently on one of the most boring topics in the universe—and never got paid. Never. When I finally summoned the nerve to phone, I was told that the personnel director had left, and there was no record of my assignment to write an annual report.

"Was the report published?" I asked.

"*A* report was published," came the answer. "You could always talk to the new personnel director, if you like."

I left a couple of messages and gave up, beaten and humiliated.

Those two experiences might have been enough to make me reconsider a writing career, but about the same time, I began selling to magazines, as in *paid*. As I gained more experience, I realized that professional editors expect to talk money, and the best time to do that is when you receive the assignment, not three months after you've turned it in.

I don't think my early experiences are all that unusual. Writers are not money people. If they were, they wouldn't have chosen writing as a career. I get depressed when I read the frequently touted figures for the average earning of freelancers in this country. Then I remind myself how deceiving those statistics can be. I know freelancers who sell one article a year, and others who sell one a week. Some writers work hard enough or get lucky enough to earn a decent living, and others earn excellent money.

Get the Free out of Freelance

You may have heard about the newest name-changing effort for freelance writers. The idea is to call yourself an "independent writer."

Although some agree that it sounds more professional, I don't think it will help writers receive more professional treatment until they become more professional in their financial dealings with publishers. *Freelance* means we are free to work for whomever we choose, not that we're willing to work for free. The problem isn't what we call ourselves. It's how we conduct business.

Before you even submit, check to see if the magazine pays on acceptance or upon publication. The former is obviously better for you. If you sell regularly to a publication, you may be more concerned with the regularity of work than with when the money arrives, but at least be aware.

Agree in Advance

Understand, in advance, what you will be paid. When the editor calls to give you an assignment or to say your article has been accepted, thank her, of course. Then ask, "Will you need an invoice?" If the answer is yes, then ask, "For what amount?" When she tells you, smile to yourself and then ask, "Does that include expenses, or do you need a separate invoice for that?" This is also a good time to discuss what rights the editor is purchasing.

Keep as many rights for yourself as possible. In accepting a columnist job with a magazine, I told the editor that I might want to include the columns for a future book. She had originally asked for all rights to the columns, but only because she didn't want to see them in competing magazines. Once she understood why I wanted the rights, she had no problem letting me retain them.

Some publications will pay your expenses, but you won't know unless you ask. When quoted a low price for an article she was writing for her local newspaper, a beginning writer asked, "What about expenses?" The editor paused, then added another

$25 to his offer. The writer's approach was a wise one. She knew what the newspaper paid, and she wanted the clip. Instead of insulting the editor about his low rates, she switched to the topic of expenses and got what she wanted.

Submit an Invoice

Unless instructed otherwise, submit an invoice as soon as possible, even with the manuscript itself. At the newspaper where I work, we juggle our budgets during busy months. Freelancers who sold us holiday articles are sometimes paid in October for articles that run in November or December.

Submit a separate invoice for each article. The editor may be able to authorize only a certain amount per month. Your invoice for $200 might go through faster than the one for $1,000.

Resell or Re-Slant?

If you're on a friendly basis with an editor, say something like, "You did a great job on this. I'd really like to sell it again." The editor may well suggest a non-competing market where you can sell it. I've been known to provide phone numbers and references to good writers, and many of my editors have extended the same courtesy to me.

A quick way to spot an amateur is the heading, usually on the right side of page 1 that notes which rights he is selling. A professional writer knows which rights the publication buys before he submits the manuscript.

Many U.S. publishers purchase First North American serial rights or first serial rights. These rights allow them to publish your work before another publisher can. The rights usually return to you after a period of time. I've been able to resell articles as soon as six months after the first publication.

Not all of these markets pay well. As I mentioned in the last chapter, one paid me only $25 per piece, but it's the only investment I know where I can get a $25 return on a postage stamp. On rare occasions, you can earn more on the second sale, and I'm certain being able to include a clip of the published manuscript with your query makes the article more credible to a prospective editor.

Check your market source book. If it says the publication purchases second serial reprint rights, this is a good target for your query and clip. Often you can sell second rights to the same publisher who bought the piece in the first place. I usually receive about half of the first price each time an article appears in one of the publisher's other magazines.

Many newspapers purchase one-time rights, because they want to be free to publish the piece in their geographical areas. Often you can sell again to publications more than fifty miles away. Some of our freelancers also sell to other newspapers in our chain.

Try not to sell all rights or all world rights. Have I done it? Yes. Would I do it again? Under the same circumstances, probably, but I do not advise it. Writing is too difficult to sell away all of your rights. Think how you'd feel when the work appeared in other publications, while you received nothing?

The same is true of work for hire. At the newspaper I have a work-made-for-hire agreement. Everything I write belongs to my employer. In return, I receive a salary, whether or not I write every day, along with the other benefits of full-time employment. I would never recommend a work-made-for-hire agreement to a freelancer. You would in essence sign away even your copyright.

This happened to me with a book sale. Here I was writing a book on writing, and I didn't know enough to check my own copyright. Then I had a disturbing conversation with the newly hired manager of the publishing firm. She suggested, during a conversation about a different matter, that the firm let English professors use my book as their own, while inserting a few chapters they had written or that someone else had written from their notes.

When I made my discomfort clear, she said, "Don't worry. You can share the byline."

I checked the contract, and sure enough, the publisher owned the copyright. I was lucky. The publisher wanted to renegotiate, and I insisted that the copyright be in my name. If my timing hadn't been right, you could probably visit your local college bookstore right now, pick up an English text with my name on it (or maybe not) and read the shell of my book wrapped around someone else's notes. Don't let it happen to you. Rights do matter.

Electronic rights are the new areas of debate, and everyone has an argument. If you're asked to sell your electronic rights, I suggest you contact the National Writers Union, which has had positive results in helping writers retain their rights. You'll find contact information in the next chapter.

Probably the best way to approach the sale of rights is with your editor, in a friendly manner that shows you are willing to negotiate. More than one editor has given me tips on what the publisher will accept. Sometimes you might be able to negotiate non-exclusive rights, where, after the initial sale, the publisher can use the piece again, with no additional compensation, and you can do the same.

As in much of the publishing business, open communication is the key. Part of being a writer is not just selling one piece and moving on, but building relationships with editors. You'll discover that when you take care of your editor, your editor will want to take care of you.

Even if you don't resell your piece, you can still re-slant it. One of my friends is an expert at re-slanting an article. I wish I could think the way she does. "When you get hungry enough, you will," she told me. "It's just the freelancer's mentality."

After talking to her through countless stories, I see how she does it. She starts when she first gets an assignment and begins her research.

"I'm working on a great piece for a medical magazine," she'll say. "I'm going to work on a kids' angle for the boys' magazine and a pet angle for the cat people."

That's the freelancer's mentality. She plans her interviews to cover more than one angle, so that she doesn't have to backtrack once she's made the sale.

Decide What You're Worth

Start for little or no pay, if you must, to acquire clips, but don't linger long in freebie land. It's bad for your self-esteem.

Ask the editor if there is any way you can be paid something, and if not, take your great clips and find a publication that pays. Once you're rich and famous, you can occasionally waive payment for worthwhile publications. While you're starting out, though, your head and your bank account need real, live cash.

Build a Relationship with Your Editors

My editors have often freely shared their frustrations and budget constraints once we established a close working relationship. If someone's budget was tight, I might agree to lower my price for once or to take part of my payment in trade. I've never had an editor take advantage of me for this offer, and my ultimate rewards have been greater than my sacrifices.

Meet your deadlines and prove yourself a reliable writer. Share your good ideas with your favorite editor first. You'll be rewarded with better assignments and often behind-the-scenes information about the publication.

When the Check's Not in the Mail

It happens. Sometimes the check doesn't materialize when you think it will. This is especially true if you needed that money yesterday. For some reason I've yet to fathom, needed funds don't appear on command for writers. That's another reason to juggle more than one assignment.

Sooner or later you're going to have to inquire about your money, and sooner is your best option. If you don't receive payment in a timely manner, call the editor and inquire as to the status of your invoice. That's what your editor would ask her boss if her paycheck didn't show up as expected.

I've never had an editor refuse to help me collect payment, and a call from an editor has more clout with the payroll department than a call from you.

If the editor held onto your invoice—if it's buried in a pile of manuscripts, your call to the editor will give her a chance to turn it in without looking unprofessional to her colleagues and to you.

If you've understood from the assignment how, as well as what, the publication pays, you should be able to note the week (although not the day) you'll be paid. If not, start those friendly calls. After two of them, you need to have a serious talk with the editor or with the payroll person. Only a truly flaky publication will try to avoid paying you, as long as you are proactive.

You, not the publisher, are the one who should take action. I once received a notice from our newspaper's payroll department that a check had been returned because it was sent to the wrong address. Two months later, I was finally able to locate the out-of-state writer.

When I asked why she hadn't gotten in touch with me, she said, "I didn't want to bother you." I owe you money, lady. Bother me.

Rarely a publication is so terrible that you need to warn other writers about it. When you encounter one, you can help others from being victimized. Some writers' publications list questionable literary agents and publishers. I've talked off-the-record with editors who, because they fear legal repercussions, don't print a fraction of what they know. Send that letter, make that phone call, but if you don't get results, keep going.

The majority of payment problems happen early in a writer's career, and many of them are based on poor communication. In time, you develop a nose and can almost smell a financially shaky publication. Thanks to the Internet, the news of those publications travels faster than it used to.

How to Write an Invoice

An invoice is an important sales tool that too many writers ignore or forget. It reminds the editor that you have a deal and that the deal won't be completed until payment is made. It also helps you keep track of your sales. When I began writing, I couldn't believe that I'd ever sell enough to have such a problem, but it happens. Assign each invoice a number. I precede the number by one or two letters. If it's my third sale to Blue Dolphin, I head the invoice BD-3. This simple system keeps me organized and paid.

Although you can find software programs for dazzling invoices, you won't impress the payroll department, whose job it is to issue checks for works purchased.

Stay away from anything that resembles fancy, cute or complicated. You'll never see editors sitting around discussing the most creative invoice they ever received. An editor-friend did tell me about a beginning writer whose invoice made her smile because of its very simplicity. It said:

"You owe me $100. Jerry."

That's almost all you need. Here is the rest.

Invoice #

Your Name
Your Street Address
Your City, State and Zip Code
Your Telephone Number
Your Social Security Number

Submitted: Today's Date

To: Editor's Name
Publication's Name
Publication's Street Address
Publication's City, State and Zip

For: Freelance article
Title
Word Count and issue appearing, such as March 1999 issue (if you know)

Amount due: $

Terms: Net 30 days (or whatever your agreement
with the editor)

Thank you. (Optional)

The Rules of Doing Business

64. Resolve to be as professional in handling the
    business side of your job as you are in handling
    the creative side.

65. Agree, in advance, on the amount and terms
    of payment.

66. Ask about expenses.

67. Understand your rights and try to retain as many
    as possible.

68. Submit separate invoices as soon as possible.

69. Try to resell or re-slant articles.

70. Do not sign a work-made-for-hire agreement for
    a freelance job.

71. Seek help in negotiating electronic rights.

72. Communicate with your editor regarding rights.

73. Don't work for free.

74. Take care of your editor and expect the same
    treatment.

75. Inquire if a payment is late.

76. If you must, seek outside help resolving payment.

77. Submit clear, concise — not dazzling — invoices.

What's Next?

Now is the time to look into professional organizations and other groups for writers. Can you join the world of networking and still respect yourself in the morning?

CHAPTER 7

Networking Without the Net

Just remember, we're all in this alone.

LILY TOMLIN

Back in the early 1980s, I was invited by a much more established writer to attend a business luncheon with her. When I inquired what type of luncheon, she responded with that glib vagueness practiced by Amway and vitamin-supplement pushers. Uncomfortable but unable to refuse, I went to the Downtown Club and sat silently as our luncheon group introduced themselves and dealt out their business cards.

One sold insurance, as I recall, another real estate, and still another was a couples/career counselor, presumably looking for patients on either front. This luncheon was a professional leads group traveling incognito. Such groups allow only one of each profession into their fold, the writer explained. She was the official novelist, but if I joined, I could be the official editor.

Maybe I was too judgmental. How many referrals is an editor going to receive from a bunch of sales people and one paperback writer, after all? And if I really did get one, what would I do with it? Could I charge the real estate agent for editing his firm's next radio commercial? Might I rewrite the couples/career counselor's unfocused brochure? You can see why I could hardly wait to get away from those smiling networkers and their so-called free lunch.

Most of us who write for a living are too independent for the old *quid pro quo* type of networking that did and maybe still does work for numerous insurance agents, employment recruiters and CPAs. Being on either end of tit-for-tat networking is too political for us.

If we are to believe the psychologists who study writers, we in this business started out as lonely kids. We read, and reading led us to thinking about the magic of words. The very act is solitary, which is why so many of us value and refuse to squander our connections to other writers.

Network is defined as, "an open fabric or structure in which cords, threads or wires cross at regular intervals. A system made up of interconnecting parts."

The first definition bothers me because of the term, "regular intervals." There's nothing regular about when and how writers connect. Your path may cross mine today, and mine may cross the path of your best friend five years from now. There is no way that we can keep a ledger or expect a cross-referral system from each other. We're too busy writing.

Yet we need contact as much or more than we need contacts.

Consider Conferences

Writing conferences are valuable for writers who are just beginning, as well as established writers who appear as speakers. The conference atmosphere is conducive to unstructured networking, impromptu dinners and coffee sessions at daybreak. I count among my dear friends a novelist in Colorado, an essay-writer in Albuquerque, and a screenwriter in Ft. Bragg, Calif., and I met them all at writers' conferences.

For me, it's an opportunity to interact with others, whatever their skills or credits, who love this word business as much as I do. Through them, I'm able to rediscover the eager writer still living within me.

If you're looking for contacts, you'll find them at conferences as well. Most major publishers don't accept unsolicited submissions, yet one of my students connected with an editor for a major house at a conference. The publisher purchased the student's unwritten manuscript for $50,000.

I hear as many deals taking place behind the scenes as I do during the scheduled agent/editor sessions. Agents, editors, publishers, talk shop. At a conference, we talk to each other. As a result, we pick up industry gossip, make professional contacts for later and can often shop our own writing projects.

Speaking at a conference gives you a chance to articulate what you know, to yourself, as much as anyone else. It also gives you an opportunity to give back to other writers. No group you've ever addressed is more receptive to a sincere speaker than a group of hungry-for-knowledge writers.

They're also perceptive. If you're there to scam or pitch your own projects, you'll find your sessions pretty empty and your name at the bottom of the evaluation sheet. At one conference, attendees who paid close to $500 to attend, were greeted in the main conference room at 7:30 AM with loud music and a way-too-energetic woman in a red leotard urging them to, "Stretch, come on, move." The woman was hawking, for a mere $20, a gigantic red rubber band for stretching, the type you can purchase for $5 or get from a physical therapist at no charge. Those attending were not amused. Writers can smell a scam, even at 7:30 in the morning.

If you don't care about helping others connect, a conference is probably not for you. If you do, send a note or e-mail to the chair person to get scheduled for the following year's event. You can find information online or in writers' magazines such as *Poets & Writers* and *Writer's Digest*. Submit a list of publications and suggested topics for speaking. If you've taught writing classes, mention that as well.

Those Who Can . . .

Teaching a writing class is not for everyone. I still can't believe that it's for me. It doesn't pay well, and if you do it right, you use time that could be spent writing. Many students think they own you away from class as well as in.

Why teach? Probably for the same reason you write—because you can't help it. For me, it's a way of giving back, of saving others all the time I wasted trying to find a mentor. I love my students, and I get more from the synergy of my workshop than I give. I actually write more and better when my classes are in session.

Teaching will provide you an opportunity to talk about nothing but writing one afternoon or evening a week, and by editing and evaluating your students' work, you'll learn a great deal about your own.

Every once in a while, you will connect with a wonderful writer who will become a wonderful friend. You may even be blessed with a group like my advanced workshop, where every writer gets published, and class members are like family in the best sense of the word.

If you've ever searched for a writing class, you already know that most leave something to be desired. Take a look at the writing teachers in your community. How many can support themselves on their writing incomes? How many are really turning out professional, published writers? If you care, and if you know your subject, you'll be welcomed by grateful students.

Look into requirements at the local adult school, community college, or university. Then focus on your passion. Don't try to teach something just because it's a popular subject. Go with something you love. You'll already be aware of the best authorities on the subject and whether or not you agree with them.

Picture the type of student you can help and write up a sample blurb. One of my students teaches a senior citizen memoir-writing class. That's her interest. Another leads a group of writers of children's books. I teach writing for publication and offer other classes in novel writing and narrative nonfiction.

Although you may later want to teach a private class, working for a school will expose you to the writers in your community, and it will promote you at no personal expense. There's also something legitimate about teaching in a classroom versus at your dining room table. It makes you more accessible to a more diverse group of people.

Make New Friends

Your writing friend doesn't have to live in the same city or state. If you admire something someone has written, send a note. Of course, you're thinking. Johnny Megabucks is going to love hearing how much I liked his last novel. Maybe so. With Web sites, such contact is much less intrusive.

Refer a writer you respect for a speaking job or an assignment, whether or not this person is a close friend. You can make the difference in someone's life, in this industry that operates on word of mouth and referral.

Give a talented beginner a chance. Maybe it's a job that you don't have the time to do; maybe it's a group you wish you had joined sooner. Passing along a tip costs you nothing.

Maybe you have an old client whose pay rate is too low for you now. It worked once, and it can work for another writer. Instead of turning down the next assignment, suggest someone else.

When I hear and/or meet a talented speaker at a conference, I refer that person to directors at other conferences where I speak. I've made such a habit of this that some directors actually phone me for referrals. I was keynote speaker at one conference where a tiny knot of speakers kept to themselves (behind the table where their books were for sale) and didn't mix with those attending. Their body language and facial expressions made it clear that they had no desire to meet beginning writers who could do them no good.

One of the chilliest approached me after my talk and pressed a business card into my hand. "You speak at some high-powered conferences, and I'd obviously like to do that," she said. Stunned, I mumbled that I would hold onto her card. I didn't, but I haven't forgotten her name or the way she conducts herself at a conference.

Keep the Old

If you're on a book deadline, as I was recently, your writer friends will understand when you send a group e-mail. They'll support you with messages like, "You don't have to answer this," or "Get back when you can," or in my case, "You go, girl."

When you aren't on deadline, save time for your writer

friends. We need each other. Only other writers understand how crazy you are. Would you tell a normal person that you send out self-addressed envelopes, complete with postage, so that your manuscripts can be returned to you?

Respect the time of other writers. Don't be a time hog. Preface each phone call by asking, "Are you working?" or, "Is this a good time for you?" Learn and honor the writer's schedule.

Don't Get Clubbed

I once attended the meeting of a local writers' club, and by the time we left, I'd been asked to serve as president. Even then I knew, to paraphrase Groucho Marx, that I wanted no part of a club that wanted me as a leader. I was searching for direction; I didn't want to direct. That's the problem with most local clubs for writers. Anyone can join, and anyone can lead. Worse, they're not productive.

Look at your local group, and I'll bet you see very few officers publishing anything. They're too busy being clubbed. They have meetings to attend, members to recruit, speakers, dues. If you're looking for an excuse not to make it as a writer, getting clubbed ranks right up there with marriage and reproduction in the excuse department. Exceptions exist, although they are usually closed critique groups.

You could gain more by joining a national organization. National Writers Union, Southwest Writers Workshop, Editorial Freelancers Association, Society of American Business Editors & Writers, Society of Professional Journalists and Writer's Guild of America are all groups I support. I belong to several of them, and I've never felt pressured to pass out handshakes or business cards.

In the 1960s, Bishop James Pike said the church must decide

if it were to be a club or a cause. The same is true of writers' groups today. All too often, writers' clubs are like those nets where every thread, wire and person crosses at regular intervals. Many of us have been tangled in such nets. Causes are different.

Whatever our diverse philosophy or genre, we share the same cause — love of and respect for the written word. We want to connect with others who experience what we do, separately, in the act of communicating our images on paper. I believe that we value not networking, but connection. Connecting means supporting the cause instead of promoting the club. A professional writer values his or her connections and honors them, and not just because it might help bring in the next sale.

With apologies to Lily Tomlin, we writers are all in this alone — together. A few years ago, a novelist friend of mine tried to quit smoking and couldn't. When he complained to his agent that it was affecting his writing, she said she knew another writer who had been through it. My friend received an encouraging telephone call the next week. The caller was Stephen King. Alone and together. That's the network — not regular at all, but very much connected.

Organizations for Writers

American Medical Writers Association
160 Fifth Avenue, Suite 625
New York, NY 10010
(212) 645-2368

American Society for Journalists and Authors
1501 Broadway, Suite 302
New York, NY 10036
(212) 997-0947

Editorial Freelancers Association
71 West 23rd Street
New York, NY 10010
(212) 929-5400

Education Writers Association
1331 H. NW, Suite 307
Washington, DC 20036
(202) 637-9700

National Association of Science Writers
PO Box 294
Greenlawn, NY 11740
(516) 757-5664

National Writers Union
113 University Place
6th Floor
New York, NY 10003
(212) 254-0279

Outdoor Writers of America
2017 Cato Avenue, Suite 101
State College, PA 16801

Society of American Business Editors & Writers
University of Missouri School of Journalism
76 Gannett Hall
Columbia, MO 65211
(314) 882-7862

Society of American Travel Writers
4101 Lake Boone Trail, Suite 201
Raleigh, NC 27607
(919) 787-5181

Society of Children's Book Writers and Illustrators
22736 Vanowen Street, Suite 106
West Hills, CA 91307
(818) 888-8760

Southwest Writers Workshop
1338-B Wyoming Blvd NE
Albuquerque, NM 87112
(505) 293-0303

Society of Professional Journalists
16 S. Jackson
Greencastle, IN 46135
(317) 653-3333

Writer's Guild of America (East)
555 W. 57th Street, Suite 1230
New York, NY 10019
(212) 767-7800

The Rules of Networking

78. Don't expect networking to work for you in the same way it works for business people.

79. Consider speaking at a writers' conference once you have credits and something to say.

80. Contact the conference director a year in advance.

81. Be certain that you are attending to help other writers and not just to promote yourself.

82. Investigate teaching opportunities in your community.

83. Adult schools, community colleges and universities are your best places to start.

84. Be certain that you really know and have hands-on experience in your subject.

85. Evaluate your priorities and commitment level before making a decision.

86. Send notes of praise or thanks to writers you admire.

87. Refer writers to jobs and speaking engagements.

88. Save time for your writer friends.

89. Respect the time of other writers.

90. Think twice before joining a local writers' club.

91. Think more than twice about becoming an officer in one.

92. Consider national organizations for writers.

What's Next?

Sooner or later, the nasty old rejection blues will get you down. Here are steps you can take to rescue a piece on which you're ready to give up.

CHAPTER 8

Rescue Your Writing from Rejection

It took me fifteen years to discover
that I had no talent for writing, but I couldn't give it up
because by that time I was too famous.

ROBERT BENCHLEY

Most writers give up too soon on a promising piece, and for good reason. No one likes to hear, "No," regardless of the language in which it is couched. I certainly don't. In fact, I'm the worst person to teach you how to handle rejection. What I hope to teach you is how to learn from rejection and even how to defy it.

"You shouldn't take it personally," the experts say. Well, why not? Turning down your manuscript probably isn't personal to the editor, but that rejection is certainly going to feel personal to you.

In Chapter 5, I talked about how to lessen the sting by keeping many projects in the mail at all times. I think it's dangerous for your self-esteem to push just one wonderful, labor-of-love project. To do so narrows your chances of success, and there's always a chance that this labor-of-love project isn't very good. Don't give up on it, but keep other projects out there.

Timing

Today's failed manuscript may be tomorrow's hit, but like the metaphorical tree falling in the forest, a manuscript can't be published if the editor doesn't see it. You need to keep the material you care about circulating. The quality of your writing may have nothing to do with the rejections.

You may have a good idea but not the skill to develop it. In 1998, I sold a book I first pursued in the early 1980s. The book I wrote in 1998 bore little resemblance to the one I'd visualized fifteen years earlier.

The content of your manuscript might be what is keeping it from selling right now. A novelist friend on her sixth book, just sold her first. The controversial topic that held it back a decade ago is gaining the author a reputation for her handling of cutting-edge material.

Even if they are not controversial, certain types of books sell better at different times. You can try to second-guess the trends, or you can do as I do and write what is in your heart and head.

I wrote my first book in 1992, not a good time for books about writing. On my first try, I landed an agent, from a top New York firm, who believed in the book and worked hard to sell it. Finally his enthusiasm dwindled and died, along with my hopes.

"It's the market," he told me. "Books about writing just don't sell these days."

I parted company with him as amicably as one can with a messenger of unpleasant truth. To console myself, I wrote and sold numerous freelance pieces. Yet, in spite of what my erstwhile agent had said about the market, I continued to see and purchase new books on writing.

I also continued speaking at writing conferences, where I often heard the irksome questions, "Don't you have a book out? Where can I buy it?"

As I learned more about the writing industry, I revised the book over the years, and at the suggestion of a friend, submitted it to a small house that publishes college textbooks. It was published in 1995, a far different book than the one my former agent had tried to sell. If I'd given up for good the way I wanted to after my agent did—that book would never have been published.

Does this sound like you? Have you written something you and others believe in? Have you been rejected, defeated? Do those once-proud pages wilt beneath the sheets in your linen closet now? Are you ready to throw in the proverbial towel?

If so, wait just one minute. Don't make the same mistakes I did. If you believed in the manuscript once, you can believe in it again, and you can fix it, if you have to.

Reputable Doesn't Necessarily Mean Big

If you've sent your essay to the *New Yorker* and can't think of another deserving market, get creative. If you're writing, you should also be reading. What publications do you enjoy? How many buy from freelancers? Go back to Chapter 2 and review the many ways you can locate a publication.

The same is true with marketing a book. Investigate independent publishers. Read the advertisements in industry publications, making note of the titles that sound like yours. Who is publishing them? Visit your local bookstore. Take notes. Who is publishing your type of book?

Sell Yourself in Pieces

Take a look at that large, sprawling article. Yes, you love it, but maybe a piece of it might stand on its own. I've sold profiles of writers taken from longer articles. You could do the same with just about any topic.

While you're marketing the first piece, try sending queries using a different slant. If the article is for a tennis magazine, think about giving it a strictly women's or young-adult focus.

I've also sold essays or articles taken from a then-unpublished book. These sales kept me going over the months and years the book was systematically rejected.

The Pros and Cons of Contests

Some suggest entering writing contests as a way to add credibility to your work and to get it before the editor judges. In all honesty, it doesn't work that way. Few of the entries I've evaluated for major writing contests were ready for publication. If the contest has eighteen honorable mentions, your win won't sound credible to anyone who knows the quality of the average entry. A win in a contest will convince you that you do have a worthwhile project, and that's almost as important as convincing someone else.

Reputable contests, such as the annual one sponsored by the Southwest Writers Workshop in Albuquerque, offer critiques. If you read yours with an open mind, you might find out how to improve your manuscript. After three different contest judges advised her to change the title of her book, a writer friend of mine was convinced to part with the darling she had believed a perfect title.

I've seen other talented writers set back by entering contests. One received a critique sheet full of general complaints like, "Need to tighten," with no direction as to how that could be accomplished. The author was upset, and because I knew the contest coordinator, I called to complain. He asked which category, and when I told him, he groaned and said he'd had nothing but complaints in that category. My friend was given another, more helpful critique, but I worry about the writers who didn't complain, especially the beginners who won't dare to speak up.

If you get a really lousy critique, let the people in charge hear about it. The contest organizers need to know how their judges are perceived. Your complaint probably won't be the only one, and it could stop that judge from damaging other writers.

If you enter a contest, be certain you know what you want in return, beyond the prize money, that is. If there is an entry fee, be certain you know whether or not you'll receive a critique. Don't just throw out your money, hoping you can purchase publication with an entry fee.

You already know this, but just as a reminder, keep away from vanity contests that promise cash prizes and promise publication to everyone who purchases a copy of the anthology.

You can find contests listed online and in publications such as *Writer's Digest, Poets & Writers* and *ByLine* magazines.

Creating a Demand

The current buzzword is "platform." "What's her platform?" an editor will ask an agent about a writer. What it means is: How well known are you in your field? A career columnist friend of mine reaches more than a million readers. That's a strong platform, and combined with a book proposal, will undoubtably land her a contract.

Get known in your area of expertise. April Sinclair did it by giving readings in Oakland long before she convinced an agent at a writing conference to represent her coming-of-age novel, *Coffee Will Make You Black*.

I spoke at writing conferences while my first book gathered dust in my closet. One of my former students, who wrote a book on how to prevent a heart attack, teaches an adult-school class on that timely topic. A doctor friend of mine, the author of one of the many books on estrogen, lectures at women's conferences and conducts radio interviews, often for no fee.

You can do the same by lecturing or reading whenever and wherever you can get your proverbial foot in the door. Pretend, for a moment, that you're an editor. Whether buying a coming-of-age novel, or a book on writing, heart-attack prevention or estrogen, wouldn't you go with a writer with credibility, not to mention a following?

Seeking Help

If you continue to collect rejections, seek outside help. This doesn't mean you should ask your spouse to read your wonderful, much-rejected manuscript. As I'll discuss in the next chapter, your family members have an agenda—to bring you up or put you down. Besides, they don't know enough to help you.

Find a qualified professional who writes or, better yet, edits the kind of material you want to sell. Then, listen to what that person tells you. Don't make excuses. Don't be defensive. Bite your tongue if you even feel like uttering those damning words, "But I wrote it that way because...." Give yourself twenty-four hours to sleep on the comments. If you still don't agree, or if you aren't certain this is the right person for you, find another.

Many writers' associations provide member critiques for nominal fees. If you work with someone locally, ask for references first. I've seen some scary people passing themselves off as editors and even believing it themselves.

While you're submitting your manuscript, continue to write and submit new ones, so that your skills and successes will be increasing as you wait.

Finally and most important, don't give up. Remember that more than ninety-five percent of everything submitted is rejected. You can't let that stop you. So the odds are against you. Sure they are, but most writers out there don't know what you've just learned. They're the reason for the ninety-five-plus percent. While they're mailing, you're revising. While they're trying to phone John Grisham's agent, collect, you're methodically working, submitting and starting new projects.

James Lee Burke is reputed to have gone thirteen years between books. When I saw a first edition of his at a used bookstore, I asked the price. "Twenty-five," the store owner said.

A little steep, I thought, but it was hardcover, and I do love Burke. "I'll take it," I replied.

The owner smiled and said, "That's twenty-five *hundred*."

Twenty-five hundred dollars for a book it took thirteen years to publish? Such miracles are only possible when you refuse to give up. Regardless of the trends and the current market, the right story, article, poem or novel will find a home sooner or later.

Buy a bottle of Domaine Chandon or a pint of Ben and Jerry's ice cream. Every time you look at that bottle, that carton, remind yourself that this is your reward, to be consumed only upon the occasion of selling your manuscript. Then, continue taking the steps to make that happen.

Remember the words of Richard Bach. "A professional writer is an amateur who didn't quit."

Somewhere out there, is an editor who wants to pay real, live dollars for what you have written. Your job is to connect, and you are the only one who cares enough to create that connection. If you give up, it won't happen, and if you let rejection stop you, it most definitely won't happen.

Planning on how you could blow up the publishing house really isn't very productive behavior. Try to keep each rejection in perspective, and don't let it make you crazy.

If there is one writer who hates rejection more than I, it is my friend Sheree Petree, author of *Rubber Knees, A Telephone Company Mystery*, which won the Dark Oak First Novel Award in 2001. When Sheree first joined my workshop, she was employed writing and producing a local television program. But that wasn't *real* writing, Sheree explained. Rejections caused her to doubt herself, stop writing, and stop communicating even with those closest to her.

"What's wrong?" I asked when I phoned her during one of these funks.

"Oh, nothing."

"How's the novel coming?"

"Not so well. Maybe I should stick to TV."

"You get a rejection?"

"Yeah, from an agent. I can't even bear to open the envelope."

"Open it now," I said. "Read it to me."

I heard the shuffling of papers. "I knew it," she said. "They sent it back. Wait, there's a note." Slowly, she began to read. "We regret to inform you that (the agent) passed away last month, and thus we are returning your submission."

Sheree had been making herself miserable over a rejection from a dead agent. Don't do this. Be a finisher. Hang in there long enough, and you'll find that you really can rescue your writing from that murky sea of rejection.

The Rules of Surviving Rejection

93. Know that there are many reasons for rejection, only one of which is quality.

94. Your manuscript's appeal and your skills will change with time.

95. Seek out smaller publications and independent publishers.

96. Sell pieces of your article or book.

97. Enter a contest, but only after you're certain it's a reputable one.

98. If you receive an insulting or unhelpful critique, complain.

99. Try to get known in your field while you're trying to sell your manuscript.

100. Find a qualified professional whom you can pay to criticize your manuscript.

101. Don't be defensive or try to explain why you wrote it as you did.

102. Don't give up.

What's Next?

There is life after publication, and it may not be at all what you expected.

CHAPTER 9

Life After Publication

To love oneself is the beginning of a
life-long romance.

OSCAR WILDE

I f you think you had problems launching your writing career,
don't expect publication to solve them. True, it will solve some
problems, money, for starters. You still won't be able to buy that
second home on the coast or in the mountains, so that you can
join the select few who use "summer" as a verb. More to the
point, you'll still have to scramble for assignments. You'll still
have to prove yourself to each new editor — with one big difference — you're a published writer.

Love Thy Editor

Do not forget that all of this good fortune was due to one or
two people and their belief in your work. Keep and nurture
these original contacts. We'd all love to bounce from the *Pipsqueak*

Gazette to the *New Yorker,* but that's a pretty broad jump. If you've found an editor who loves you at the *Gazette,* enjoy the attention and learn what you can from him.

Each time he gives you an assignment, remember to ask how he sees the finished piece. What is the piece he visualizes? What is the focus? When is the piece due? With that in mind, you can continue to plan and grow as a writer.

The Plan, According to You

Look at your goals for the next year. Consider your most important goal first (Rewrite and sell that much-rejected novel; publish an article in a top magazine). Next, look at three to five secondary goals. (1) Prepare a new book proposal. (2) Sell an article. (3) Market your essay.

For each goal, you need a plan, a written one. You will finish the novel rewrite by March 30 and send it to X numbers of publishers each month. You will prepare the book proposal by June 2 and mail it by June 10. You will have three articles in the mail by July 20. You will take Labor Day weekend to write essays and edit those you've already written.

Now you have goals, you need plans to reach them and deadlines for those plans. Nothing in life would happen without deadlines. Publications would never get printed, never get written, for that matter.

Try to estimate how much time each project will require. Do you know how much you can produce in a day? You should. Don't gauge it by your day job, complete with coffee/lunch breaks and conversation with coworkers.

Try timing yourself on a day when all you do is write toward a specific deadline for a specific piece. The total will surprise you. Try not to overcommit so that you'll still have time to work on something you love.

The Cookie Monster and Other Temptations

Another concern you'll have as a freelancer can be summed up in one word—gifts. Is it appropriate to send a gift to your editor, and if so, what type? Because of my day job as an editor, I can tell you than an inappropriate remembrance will indeed make the editor remember you, but not in the way you would like. A silver Tiffany pen engraved with my name and delivered to my desk did not endear me to any of my coworkers and was too excessive.

In the newspaper business, the motto used to be, "If you can't eat it or smoke it, don't accept it as a gift." Now that no one smokes, most gifts are limited to chocolates and fruit.

I've heard some editors, including one from a large publishing house, say that they like to receive gifts—if they feel there are no strings attached. How can there not be? When you send a gift, you may be saying thanks for past favors, but you're certainly putting your bid in for future favors as well.

If you decide to send a gift to an editor, don't do it while that person is considering a manuscript from you. Wait until a holiday, then send something that can be shared with the staff, and don't spend a lot of money. One of my freelancer friends makes points with editors by sending a plastic bucket filled with various types of cookies during the Christmas holidays.

I do not send anything to an editor until I've worked with that person long enough to consider her a friend. When I know her well enough to know when her birthday is and how she plans to spend it—if I know I'd send the gift whether or not she were my editor, then I feel comfortable. Remember, public relations people send gifts. Friends send gifts. If you're not one, you're the other. If you're not certain, don't do it. Your present won't buy publication, and it could embarrass the editor. Work instead on earning her respect by the way you handle your assignments.

The Three Big Lies

Once you're established as a freelancer, your name will find its way onto any number of mailing lists. Mine certainly has. Another one arrived in the mail recently, this time trying to entice me to visit the Cayman Islands.

"Our mission also includes encouraging and facilitating in-person media visits," read the letter from the Caymans' new public relations firm. "Because the Cayman Islands include so many unique and varied sites, we would appreciate the return of the enclosed questionnaire which will enable us to tailor story ideas that are relevant to your interests and readers' needs."

I glanced at the questionnaire, all the way from "Artisans and crafts" to "Romance, honeymoon packages" and "Scuba diving & snorkeling." The italicized type at the bottom read, "If you would like to be contacted in the near future to discuss arrangements for a customized media visit to the Cayman Islands, check here or phone."

Free lunches, free trips, cushy freelance jobs. They're the three big lies of journalism.

When I first began writing, I was impressed with other writers I met who were always jetting off to the Bahamas or touring the Napa Valley on some public relations firm's tab. They got wined and dined. They visited exotic locales. *Someday,* I thought.

I soon noticed that these writers didn't publish for long or in very reputable publications. The free trips exist all right. Accepting one will usually destroy your credibility, right along with most markets for the resulting article. "Sponsored" is the word often used to describe these freebies. Many editors want to know in advance if you've taken one, and if you have, you probably won't get the assignment.

Too many dream jobs look better going in than going out. There's nothing exciting about ordinary assignments and routine payment from editors you've known and with whom you've worked for years. The dependability factor can make those jobs look pretty appealing after a few of the so-called cushy ones have come and gone.

I was surprised when a colleague with questionable work ethics landed such a job from an airline magazine.

"It's like stealing," he said. "I just rewrite the press releases, and they're paying me $400 per article."

Too much, I thought.

"Aren't you doing any interviews?" I asked.

"If I get a chance, I will, but I don't have to. I've gotten two more assignments for next month."

It wasn't stealing. It was stupid. I wished my colleague well and silently hoped the new car he'd just purchased wasn't based on his faith in this easy job.

As I arrived at work less than a month later, I found him at his desk, clutching a copy of the day's newspaper, his face the color of chalk. The airline had declared bankruptcy. He received payment for only one of his articles.

Such experiences teach us to value the reliable as well as the excessive. Yet, we've all written articles that cost more to research than what we earned for them. We tell ourselves the experience and the clips are worth it, and maybe they are, when we're just starting. At some point, we've had enough.

Perhaps the first question to ask an editor who doesn't accept sponsored articles should be, "Then do you pay travel expenses?" If that doesn't work, you might investigate the good old press rate. It's usually far lower than regular rates but acceptable to more editors.

I write better and breathe easier when I'm free from expectation, my own or anyone else's. Although I do less traveling than the writer/editors who accept trips, I wouldn't want to trade places with them. I can't kid myself into thinking I'd do the same work if I felt in any way indebted. I want the words on the page to come from me and not from my sponsor.

Subtle Sabotage

The day you see your words in print will and should feel like the newest national holiday. At this moment, you know something about yourself you might never have realized before. You're a finisher. Maybe you dropped out of Boy Scouts, Job's Daughters, high school, college, graduate school, marriage, career, parenthood. I'm not claiming that getting published can fix most of the mistakes you've made in your life, but I've do believe that it can change your perspective on most of them.

If you're anything like most of the people I teach and for whom I edit, your family and friends probably weren't all that happy that you decided to become proactive in your desire for a writing career. Such concern usually shows up in comments like, "I just don't want you to get hurt, dear." "Don't get your hopes up too high, in case something goes wrong." "Do you really have the qualifications to write about that?"

How they react after you publish will help you determine where they are in their own lives as well as how equipped they are to be friends with anyone. How many people do you know who possess both talent and follow-through? Oh, sure, there was your aggressive sibling, smarter than you for sure, but after that horrible college/spouse/career, never developed his/her potential.

And don't forget your parents or your first love. Great potential there, too, for writing—what was it?—poetry, country tunes, political speeches? Turns out that it doesn't matter. Sibs don't matter, parents don't matter, former loves don't matter, and most of all, potential does not matter. Except it matters to them, now that you're living proof that it's possible to do more than talk.

If you'd lived your life under that waning streetlight of potential, what would you do when someone else, close to, even below you in the hierarchy of your imagination, scored? Would you applaud, or would you do whatever it takes, including sabotage, to protect your most intimate image of you?

"You got how much for that? After all that work?"

"Who's taking care of the kids while you're doing that stuff?"

"No wonder we didn't see you at the meeting yesterday."

Or the down-and-dirty: "Can't you even get a part-time job?"

The answers to all the these questions is, "none of your business." If you want to continue a relationship with this person, say, "I'm doing what I love, and I'm happy." Don't expect this to placate your critics though. If there's anything an inactive hates more than a successful proactive, it's a happy one.

One of the students in my beginning class was married with two children by the time she realized what I've just told you, and it took a near-failure for her to see it.

While still in that first seven-week class, Vicki submitted an essay in our local newspaper. The editor loved it and wanted to run it on a Saturday op-ed page. Vicki was both excited and tense when she announced the fact in class.

"Which Saturday will it be out?" I asked that night.

"They want to run it right away," she said, "as soon as I go in to have my photo taken."

I heard the trouble in her voice. She had the go-ahead. She needed only to pose for a photograph. "What's stopping you?" I asked.

She squirmed. "I have this cold sore. Besides…"

"What?"

"It's my mother," she said. "Her birthday's two Saturdays from now, and she wants it to be published on her birthday."

Once she'd spoken the words, Vicki shook her head, and I saw the realization in her face. "Oh no," she said. "I can't believe I'm still letting her do this to me."

Here on the eve of her victory, her first publication, her mother was trying to steal the show with something as insignificant as a birthday, of all things. How could when she happened to be born begin to compare to her daughter's realized success? It couldn't, of course, but the old lady used what she had. So great was the good daughter's guilt that she'd even managed to develop a cold sore to give herself a chance to stall success.

Other times with other writers, the endings aren't as positive as Vicki's. I can't tell you how many writers on the verge of success decide that they need to take a short sabbatical (an oxymoron for sure) or to simply spend more time with Dad and Mom. Besides, little Joey just entered third grade. I can write anytime, but what kind of parent would I be if I didn't drive him to school every day?

No, you must write now, and regardless of gender, didn't your spouse agree to drive little Joey to school? What changed? Oh, that's right. You either got published, or better yet, you're on deadline for an article. Now, little Joey becomes your responsibility, your albatross, you bad parent, you.

I had one student whose husband followed her to class, because he was convinced I was a man. She fictionalized her abusive marriage and sold the piece to a confession magazine. Another one screamed at her spouse that he was living in a fantasy world by pursuing writing. They are no longer a couple. Subtle sabotage is the worst because it can leave you doubting yourself. Maybe you really are selfish. And what if you are? Would you rather be selfless, without self?

One of my students tells a story of a father who is trying to read the evening paper while dealing with interruptions from his young son. Finally, he tears a photograph of the world from the paper and cuts it into pieces. "Here's a puzzle for you," he says. "Put it together, and then we'll play." To his surprise, the son returns at once, the puzzle back in one piece.

"How did you do that?" the father demands.

"It was easy," his son says. "On the back of the page was a photo of the man. Once I put the man together, the world fell into place."

Once you take care of *you*, the rest of your world will fall into place. Not everyone will resent your success, but you may be surprised at how many needy people you have in your life. You'll need to teach them to respect your deadlines and to treat your writing like the real job that it is. Make it clear that when you're working, you won't accept phone calls or visitors. Most will understand. Think twice about the ones who don't.

How to Know When You've Arrived
(And How to Get There)

You've arrived as a freelancer when:

1. The editor calls you with ideas.

2. They spell your name right.

3. Your deadlines outnumber your rejection slips.

4. They give you the publication's Fed Ex billing number and actually expect you to use it.

5. The check that was supposed to be in the mail really is.

You get there by:

1. Pitching good, focused ideas, regardless of how many times you've sold to the editor.

2. Continuing to work with them when they spell your name wrong, leave it out entirely or make any of the stupid mistakes editors are allowed at least four times per lifetime.

3. Collecting rejection slips early in your career, using the Rule of Twelve, Rule of Two Hundred Ten or your own rule. Also by cherishing every deadline like the gift that it is. Don't put it off or otherwise abuse it. Remember, more than ninety-five percent of the freelancers who queried the same day you did would love to have that deadline you're worrying about.

4. Earning it. Fed Ex numbers, like telephone and travel expenses, come under the heading of perquisites, and perks are earned an article, a sale, at a time. Include the SASE until you are invited not to — or until the editor stops sending them.

5. Persevering. Writing isn't just what you do. It's what you are. Once you're consistently writing, editing, marketing, and occasionally, eating and sleeping, of course, the money will come.

Self-Sabotage

Be on the lookout for anything that resembles self-sabotage. If you're always running late, if you feel the need to take a nap when you should be working on the article that is due tomorrow, you could be trying to shoot yourself in the proverbial foot. Ask yourself what's frightening you. Fear of success? Feelings that you don't deserve or aren't good enough to be a writer?

It's as if there's a voice on your shoulder whispering in your ear that you can't do it. I named mine Mrs. Delp after a former teacher of mine. The enemy is less frightening when you personalize it. My students and I now say "Delp" when we mean sabotage by others or by ourselves. "I delped myself the other night," a workshop member might say. "Convinced myself I had to pay bills before I sat down at the computer."

It helps to have a writer friend to whom you can confess. No one else, regardless of how well-meaning, knows the anxiety of sitting before a blank screen, not because it's your hobby, but because it's your job.

In the writer's world, there are not enough helpers and too many delpers. Only another writer will understand when you confess that you cleaned the toilets and all of the closets in your home that you're procrastinating about a deadline. Only another writer can make a similar confession and order you back to work.

Try not to be hard on yourself. Your first draft doesn't have to be perfect, and if you inflict that expectation on yourself, you'll do anything to avoid facing the work. Tell yourself that it's just a first draft and that you can fix it later.

As a writer, you'll encounter demons you never knew you had, and you can exorcise those demons as well. Just as you learn to spot the games others are playing, you can, in time, recognize the games you're trying to play with yourself.

The Rules to Life after Publication

103. Continue building relationships with the editors who helped you get started.

104. Make a plan of your writing goals and include deadlines.

105. Be cautious in giving gifts to editors.

106. Don't believe in the free lunch, free trip or cushy freelance job.

107. Beware of subtle sabotage from friends and loved ones and self-sabotage.

108. Refuse to feel guilty.

109. Don't demand that your first draft be perfect.

110. Find a writer who will offer support and for whom you can do the same.

111. Take care of you, and the world will fall into place.

What's Next?

The Ultimate Rule.

CHAPTER 10

The Ultimate Rule

Writing is a dog's life,
but the only life worth living.

GUSTAVE FLAUBERT

So now you have them, the rules I would share with any free-lancer coming to me for advice—all but one rule, that is. This one was summed up by best-selling novelist Nancy Taylor Rosenberg when she spoke at the 1995 Southwest Writers Conference in Albuquerque. Rosenberg was still receiving nasty rejections for *Mitigating Circumstances* after the money she received up front for the book was in the bank.

In speaking of her own difficult road to success, she told the audience, "You gotta want it, and you gotta want it bad."

And that's the final rule. If you don't truly want to be a writer, you'll find other—and probably saner—things to do with your life.

Writing, as you probably already suspect, is more than just a job. It is something you will never really leave at the office, something that will give a great deal to you and require a great deal from you. The secret? You gotta want it, and you gotta want it bad. And I think it helps a whole lot if you love it, as well.

Getting started as a freelancer will require sacrifices and juggling of priorities. Dinner will be late or not at all. No one will believe in you at first, except possibly your best friend, who may be lying. The people who claim to love you will find countless reasons to steal your writing time. You could earn more money doing anything else for a living.

But you don't want to drive a truck, teach school or sell vitamin supplements to your friends. You're willing to pay the price, both personal and professional, while you get established and learn your trade. You're a writer. Okay, then.

Follow the rules in this book. Ignore the ones that don't work for you, but check back now and then to be sure that they still don't.

A few parting tips:

- Be good to the writer in you. Give it time and respect.
- Know that writing will get easier, and you will get better.
- Have faith in yourself, and have faith in your faith.
- Time will take care of the rest.

All the Rules

1. Don't expect any book, mentor or guardian angel — regardless of what they promise or how much you pay them — to teach you how to make millions as a writer.

2. Know that most writers who sell on a regular

basis do so because they have learned the rules of connecting with and working with editors.

3. Learn how to write. Invest in and practice using a dictionary and style book.

4. Try to aim for paying markets. Writing is a business. You're providing a product, and you need to be paid for it.

5. Expect hard work as the price you pay for being a writer, and don't give up. Selling your freelance writing is (there's that word again) doable.

6. Put yourself on the editor's side of the desk. What are your needs now?

7. Go for the deadline, even if it's ridiculous and conflicts with earlier plans. Remember that most writers won't.

8. Enjoy the rush of deadline addiction, but don't let your story dry out and die.

9. Deliver the number of words you promised. If you must pad (with sidebars) or delete, do it. Anticipate, in advance, that worst-case scenario.

10. Before you criticize articles you could write better, see what works for them.

11. Be dependable.

12. Address everything you submit to a real human not to "Editor."

13. Don't get too creative with your letterhead. Save that for what you write beneath it.

14. Avoid squirrel stickers and parchment paper, and seriously consider if you want to refer to yourself as *Jane Doe, Freelance Writer* on your business card.

15. Connect with an editor through a referral, a self-referral, Internet query, writers' conference, and don't believe the Perfect Query Myth.

16. Practice the six rules of query.

17. Send the manuscript, and not the query, whenever possible.

18. Practice the quirky Rule of Twelve or your own quirky rule. Just keep many manuscripts in the mail at all times.

19. Approach editors as human first. Most of us are.

20. Start your article when it's assigned, even if the deadline is far in the future.

21. Don't assume the source will be available at the last minute.

22. Determine in advance if you should find your own sources.

23. Also inquire about length and focus of the piece.

24. Investigate the possibility of finding sources online.

25. Although the Internet is fine for research, don't mistake an online chat for an interview.

26. Include a list of sources and contact information with the manuscript.

27. Conduct a telephone interview.

28. Take notes as direct quotes.

29. Write as you go, from the first interview on.

30. Copy the publication's format, right down to the subheads.

31. If possible, give your story time to simmer.

32. If asked for a rewrite, comply.

33. If you disagree with the editing job, don't expect it to improve with future articles. Move on to another editor, another publication.

34. Invite but don't expect feedback.

35. Let the editor know that you're available for future assignments.

36. Understand that everyone needs revision.

37. If possible, put some time between you and the finished manuscript.

38. Kill your literary darlings.

39. Think *you,* not *me.*

40. Omit *etc.,* unspecific language, and seriously consider the effectiveness of your lead.

41. Avoid trendy words or terms.

42. Learn and avoid common editing errors.

43. Eliminate orphan quotes.

44. Also eliminate excessive exclamation points, colons, semicolons, ellipses.

45. Remember that no punctuation mark is wrong all of the time. However, if you see yourself repeating one mark or sliding into one style; this is the time to consider how much the mark/style may limit you.

46. Avoid using too many capital letters.

47. Don't be a jargon junkie.

48. Rework passive constructions.

49. Yank most adjectives and adverbs.

50. Vary the lengths of your sentences.

51. Follow the style of the publication.

52. Learn the rules of grammar, but don't take this accomplishment too seriously.

53. Check your mailbox and open every letter, especially the ones that don't look as if they contain money.

54. Try to include the "X" factor in anything you write.

55. When you don't hear back, find out where you stand.

56. Write a follow-up letter and use snail mail to deliver it.

57. Once it's written, treat your brainchild like a product.

58. Practice multiple submission, and don't even consider another approach.

59. When you sell your piece, notify other markets you previously queried.

60. Conduct your queries and notifications of sales professionally, whether or not the editor deserves it.

61. Start working on your next project.

62. Consider reprint markets for your current project.

63. Remain proactive and persistent, if only because you'll feel better about yourself and about this career you've chosen.

64. Resolve to be as professional in handling the business side of your job as you are in handling the creative side.

65. Agree, in advance, on the amount and terms of payment.

66. Ask about expenses.

67. Understand your rights and try to retain as many as possible.

68. Submit separate invoices as soon as possible.

69. Try to resell or re-slant articles.

70. Do not sign a work-made-for-hire agreement for a freelance job.

71. Seek help in negotiating electronic rights.

72. Communicate with your editor regarding rights.

73. Don't work for free.

74. Take care of your editor and expect the same treatment.

75. Inquire if a payment is late.

76. If you must, seek outside help resolving payment.

77. Submit clear, concise — not dazzling — invoices.

78. Don't expect networking to work for you in the same way it works for business people.

79. Consider speaking at a writers' conference once you have credits and something to say.

80. Contact the conference director a year in advance.

81. Be certain that you are attending to help other writers and not just to promote yourself.

82. Investigate teaching opportunities in your community.

83. Adult schools, community colleges and universities are your best places to start.

84. Be certain that you really know and have hands-on experience in your subject.

85. Evaluate your priorities and commitment level before making a decision.

86. Send notes of praise or thanks to writers you admire.

87. Refer writers to jobs and speaking engagements.

88. Save time for your writer friends.

89. Respect the time of other writers.

90. Think twice before joining a local writers' club.

91. Think more than twice about becoming an officer in one.

92. Consider national organizations for writers.

93. Know that there are many reasons for rejection, only one of which is quality.

94. Your manuscript's appeal and your skills will change with time.

95. Seek out smaller publications and independent publishers.

96. Sell pieces of your article or book.

97. Enter a contest, but only after you're certain it's a reputable one.

98. If you receive an insulting or unhelpful critique, complain.

99. Try to get known in your field while you're trying to sell your manuscript.

100. Find a qualified professional whom you can pay to criticize your manuscript.

101. Don't be defensive or try to explain why you wrote it as you did.

102. Don't give up.

103. Continue building relationships with the editors who helped you get started.

104. Make a plan of your writing goals and include deadlines.

105. Be cautious in giving gifts to editors.

106. Don't believe in the free lunch, free trip or cushy freelance job.

107. Beware of subtle sabotage from friends and loved ones and self-sabotage.

108. Refuse to feel guilty.

109. Don't demand that your first draft be perfect.

110. Find a writer who will offer support and for whom you can do the same.

111. Take care of you, and the world will fall into place.

112. You gotta want it, and you gotta want it bad.